WORDS
THAT WIN

What to Say to Get What You Want

Also by Don Gabor

Books

HOW TO START A CONVERSATION AND MAKE FRIENDS

BIG THINGS HAPPEN WHEN YOU DO THE LITTLE THINGS RIGHT

TALKING WITH CONFIDENCE FOR THE PAINFULLY SHY

SPEAKING YOUR MIND IN 101 DIFFICULT SITUATIONS

HOW TO TALK TO THE PEOPLE YOU LOVE

Audiobooks

HOW TO START A CONVERSATION

TALKING WITH CONFIDENCE FOR THE PAINFULLY SHY

HOW TO MEET PEOPLE AND MAKE FRIENDS AT WORK

Video

TALKING WITH CONFIDENCE: A GUIDE TO STARTING, CONTINUING,

AND ENDING CONVERSATIONS

WORDS THAT WIN

What to Say to Get What You Want

DON GABOR

Prentice Hall Press

**A member of Penguin Group (USA) Inc.
375 Hudson Street
New York, New York 10014**

www.penguin.com

Prentice Hall Press edition / September 2003

ISBN: 0-7352-0342-3

Library of Congress Cataloging-in-Publication Data

Gabor, Don.
    Words that win : what to say to get what you want / Don Gabor.
        p. cm.
    Includes index.
    ISBN 0-7352-0342-3
    1. Communication in organizations. 2. Communication in management. 3. Communication
in personnel management. 4. Communication in industrial relations. 5. Interpersonal communication.
I. Title.

HD30.3.G33 2003
658.4'5—dc21

2003055259

Printed in the United States of America

10 9 8 7 6 5 4 3 2 1

*This book is dedicated to my parents,
Trude and Fred Gabor.*

*A special thanks to my wife and editor,
Eileen Cowell,
for her many ideas, suggestions and unwavering
support in writing this book.*

*I'd also like to express my gratitude to the following
people for their assistance: my agent, Sheree Bykofsky; my
attorney, Peter Fields; Tom Power; Dr. Dan Schaefer;
Susan Rabin; Bruce Tulgan; and Mike Albert.*

CONTENTS

What do making a speech, dealing with difficult coworkers, going on a first date and getting better customer service have in common? In these situations—and hundreds more like them—you need to come up with the right words at the right time to get what you want. If you are like the millions of people who become tongue-tied at meetings, miss out on promotions, feel nervous mingling at parties, clam up around the boss, say things to relatives you later regret or never win an argument, then this book is for you.

How *Words That Win* Will Help You

Words That Win offers the answer to that question and supplies the perfect words, phrases, opening lines, scenarios, along with plenty of examples to get what you want in every aspect of your life—in your career with your boss and coworkers, in your social and personal life with friends and as a consumer in the marketplace.

I use all these strategies, tips, examples and scripts everyday, so I know they work. When you use these techniques, you, too, will sound more confident, competent and poised every time you speak.

How to Use This Book

I designed *Words That Win* so you have quick answers to most situations you might encounter. The book is divided into three parts and twenty chapters. There are hundreds of hints, lists, tips and examples.

In Part I: Words That Win in Business Situations, you will learn conversational strategies, tips and skills to help you:

- Develop a poised speaking style and image.

- Hire the right people and manage a team.

- Get along with difficult clients and coworkers.

- Negotiate great job offers and better deals.

- Master public speaking.

- Convince your boss to boost your career.

- Win arguments without making enemies.

- Make more sales.

- Build a bigger and better business network.

In Part II: Words That Win in Consumer Situations, you'll discover the right words to:

- Get better customer service in stores, restaurants and hotels.

- Talk to health-care professionals so you can make better medical decisions.

- Say (and not say) to lawyers, police and judges.

In Part III: Words That Win in Social Situations, you'll find hundreds of phrases and examples of how to:

- Make small talk and be more attractive and confident at parties and other gatherings.

- Meet and get along with your neighbors.

- Make new friends and build lasting friendships.

- Have great first dates that lead to romance.

- Build relationships and improve your marriage.

- Get along better with your relatives.

Choose a Topic—Begin on Any Page You Want

Use *Words That Win* as a reference book—you do not need to read it from cover to cover to improve your ability to communicate. Just turn to a topic that interests you and immediately begin learning how to say the right thing at the right time. You will quickly discover how easy it is to reap the rewards from *Words That Win: What to Say to Get What You Want.*

PART I

Words That Win in Business Situations

CHAPTER ONE

Polishing Your Professional Communication Style

"The most valuable of all talents is that of never using two words when one will do."

—Thomas Jefferson, third U.S. president, 1743–1826

In this chapter, you will learn:
• **Five ways to sharpen your speaking style** • **Seven quick steps to a bigger and more effective vocabulary** • **Body language that projects poise and power** • **Four ways to make your coworkers like and respect you**

When the young congressman from Texas, Lyndon B. Johnson, entered President Franklin D. Roosevelt's office, he wanted to discuss his proposal for bringing electricity to the rural areas in his district. However, much to Johnson's dismay, Roosevelt talked nonstop for most of the meeting.

Frustrated yet undeterred, Johnson knew he had to adjust his communication style if he wanted to sell his idea to the president. At their next meeting, Johnson began his pitch before Roosevelt could even utter a word.

"Water, water, everywhere and not a drop to drink," Johnson spouted. "Public power everywhere and not a drop for my poor people." It then took Johnson only another few minutes to convince Roosevelt to support his project.

Your communication style—the way you talk to and influence people—can always benefit from a little extra polish. Just like politicians who focus on the smallest details of their speeches and proposals, polishing your communication style will help you choose and use the right words when you talk to people at work.

Five Ways to Sharpen Your Speaking Style

"I have noticed that nothing I never said ever did me any harm."
—Calvin Coolidge, thirtieth U.S. president, 1872–1933

A manager for a large manufacturer returned to his office after listening to the company's president drone on at a meeting. When a coworker asked what the president spoke about, the manager replied, "Well, he didn't say."

Everyone has listened to coworkers or superiors who talk and talk but never get to the point. Your ability to express your ideas, experiences, opinions and feelings set you apart from those annoying folks who ramble on endlessly before they actually decide (if they ever do) what they want to say.

If you summarize your ideas with a few pithy sentences, your coworkers will not only remember what you said, but will also respect your ideas. Here are five ways to sharpen your speaking style using well-chosen words.

I. TELL "WHAT IS IT ABOUT?" IN JUST A FEW SENTENCES

Get into the habit of telling coworkers and clients the main ideas of books and articles you have read or workshops you have attended that might interest them. The subject of your remarks can be work-related, a funny TV show or whatever else seems right for the situation and person. You can use the five journalist questions—Who? What? When? Where? or Why?—to help you summarize.

For example, if you are chatting with a coworker or client before a meeting about an upcoming sales presentation, you might say, "I attended an interesting workshop last night on the art of public speaking.

The instructor was a real pro and everyone had a chance to stand before the group and speak for three minutes about whatever he or she wanted."

If your coworker shows interest, then briefly describe something you learned or that happened that captures the essence of the workshop. If time permits, recall a few colorful details about an exercise you enjoyed or even a topic that someone spoke about that you found interesting.

2. SPEAK IN PLAIN ENGLISH WITH CONCRETE WORDS

Have you ever talked with somebody who tried to impress you with highbrow vocabulary? Were you impressed by five-syllable words that sounded as if they belonged in a doctoral thesis or national spelling bee? Probably not, because you were too busy trying to figure out what the person was talking about.

It's true that a powerful vocabulary can have a strong impact, but only if you choose relevant words that convey meaning. Instead of using fancy "five dollar words," use colorful nouns and precise verbs that "paint pictures." When you do, others will understand and remember what you say.

3. USE SHORT, STRONG SENTENCES

Long, rambling sentences that start at one end of the room and end on the other side might confuse your listener. One easy way to avoid wordy sentences is to place the subject of your sentences (nouns naming people, places and things) close to the action words or verbs. Another way to be more concise is to eliminate these three useless expressions:

Omit "the fact that." Don't say: "The fact that we are number one in sales points to the fact that . . ."

Do say: "We are number one in sales. As a result, . . ."

Omit "who is." Don't say: "Ms. Smith, who is the head of our division, will speak today."

Do say: "Ms. Smith, our division head, will speak today."

Words to the Wise

Avoid using the word "not" to modify words, and your statements will carry more punch. Here are some examples:

WEAK	POWERFUL
Not right	unfair, wrong
Not bad	average
Not expensive	inexpensive, cheap, bargain
Not interesting	boring
Did not remember	forgot

Omit "which was." Don't say: "Our annual report, which was released last month, stated that . . ."

Do say: "Our annual report, released last month, stated that . . ."

4. MAKE DIRECT STATEMENTS

I don't know about you, but I hate it when I hear people using feeble phrases like "not so bad" or "could have been better" when they really mean "bad," "mediocre" or "disappointing." If you want a professional speaking style that resonates with confidence, then tell it like it is.

5. OMIT "VERBAL TICKS"

Verbal ticks are constant repetitions of words or phrases such as, "Well," "Ya know?" "Okay?" "Yeah." "You know what I'm saying?" "Uh-huh." "Like." These empty words fill the air but do not provide listeners with additional details or ideas to which they can respond. The only response might be an echo: "Yeah, I know what you mean." Or "Okay!"

Omitting verbal ticks will clean up your conversation style and encourage people to pay more attention to what you say.

Sharpening your speaking style makes people pay attention and understand what you say. But you can increase your influence even more when you use a powerful vocabulary.

Seven Quick Steps to a Bigger and More Effective Vocabulary

"We must have a better word than 'prefabricated.' Why not 'ready-made'?"

—Winston Churchill, British statesman, 1874–1965

James Thurber, American humorist and writer, loved to tell this story when the subject of vocabulary came up during conversation. "While recovering in the hospital," Thurber said, "I asked a nurse, 'What seven-letter word has three *u*'s in it?' The woman paused and then smiled, 'I don't know, but it must be *unusual*.' "

A powerful vocabulary helps you think on your feet during a meeting, presentation or interview. However, it is not just the number of syllables or unusual usage that impresses clients, supervisors or potential employers—it is choosing just the *right* word.

Remember to use appropriate vocabulary for the people with whom you are talking. For example, you will impress computer engineers, manufacturing executives or sales people more if you use the vocabulary associated with their industry.

Here are quick ways to build a powerful vocabulary so you can come up with just the right word anytime, anyplace and with anyone.

1. LISTEN CAREFULLY TO THE WORDS COWORKERS USE

Instead of ignoring words you do not know, guess their meanings based on how they are used. If you are still unsure you can ask, "What do you mean by . . . ?"

2. STUDY THE TRADE JOURNALS

Read newspapers, magazines and books focusing on topics that interest you or your clients. The more you read about a subject, the faster your vocabulary will grow and the more comfortable you will be discussing the topic.

3. LEARN THE INDUSTRY LANGUAGE

If you are unfamiliar with a particular business or industry, read trade magazines to learn about the special vocabulary their members use.

4. LOOK UP WORDS YOU DON'T KNOW

Keep your own personal dictionary handy and immediately look up unfamiliar words. Circle the words in the dictionary you look up so when you see them again, you can review their meanings.

5. KEEP A WORD JOURNAL

Write down new words in a journal and frequently review their meanings.

6. USE VOCABULARY-BUILDING MATERIALS

Use a "new words-a-day" calendar or other vocabulary-building books, audiotapes, video tapes and vocabulary development programs. Focus on words that you find useful.

7. EXERCISE YOUR NEW VOCABULARY EVERY DAY

Practice blending new and old vocabulary into your face-to-face conversations, on the telephone, in e-mail, in memos and in letters. In other words, expand your vocabulary each time you speak and write.

Remember that clients and coworkers are most impressed when you "talk their language" and can come up with the right words without fumbling. Now that you know *what* to say, the next thing to consider is *how* you say it. That's where body language plays a critical role.

P-O-I-S-E-D Body Language Sends Confident and Powerful Nonverbal Signals

P = Position yourself
O = Open stance
I = Interact immediately
S = Shake hands
E = Eye contact

Body Language That Projects Poise and Power

"Drawing on my finest command of language, I said nothing."
—Robert Benchley, American humorist, 1889–1945

What was the decisive moment in the 1992 televised debate between then President George H. Bush Sr. and his Democratic challenger, Bill Clinton? Television cameras caught an obviously uncomfortable President Bush glancing at his watch. Many political analysts still believe that those few critical seconds contributed to George Bush Sr. losing the presidential election.

Body language—or nonverbal communication—always plays a critical role in how others interpret your messages and assess your competence. Effective body language—frequent eye contact, smiling, shaking hands, sitting or standing erect with unfolded arms—signals confidence and makes people want to communicate with you.

On the other hand, fidgeting with your hair, playing with a pen, folding your arms, chewing gum, slouching, sitting at the far end of a conference table or avoiding eye contact silently says you are nervous, indifferent, not listening and, worst of all, lacking confidence.

To enhance your body language, use the word *P-O-I-S-E*. Each letter in the word stands for body language that sends the message that you are poised and confident.

P = POSITION YOURSELF

When you are in a conference room waiting for a meeting to begin, your body language sends signals to everyone around you, not just those with whom you are chatting. Where you stand or sit and how you position yourself in relation to others can enhance your image.

If you want to be noticed, stand or sit close enough to influential coworkers and clients to engage in conversation. Studies show that leaders prefer the head or corners of tables at conferences, so the closer you are to these positions, the more authority and confidence you project.

Take care not to stand too close or too far away from the people with whom you are talking. Standing too close to a new business acquaintance may make him or her feel threatened or uncomfortable. However, standing too far away might seem like a rebuff or rejection.

Note that in small groups, most Americans feel comfortable talking at a distance of about 2 to 3 feet. In larger groups, typical standing distance is about 3 to 4 feet. Remember that "comfort zones" vary among cultures, so watch your conversational partners and adjust your distance from them accordingly.

O = OPEN STANCE

Open stance means keeping your arms unfolded. Folding your arms is one of the biggest body language mistakes you can make. With your arms folded, you present a picture of someone who is closed-minded, defensive and uptight—hardly the nonverbal signals that impress clients, coworkers or company executives.

Now you might say, "But I'm comfortable with my arms folded, and besides, I never know what to do with my hands."

Although you may feel comfortable with your arms folded, it sends the opposite signal to those around you, so uncross your arms. What can you do with your hands? Fold them in your lap or in front of you, take notes and use them to emphasize points that you make.

I = INTERACT IMMEDIATELY

I advise people attending my conversation workshops to interact with their coworkers and clients before a meeting because silence can be deadly. The longer you silently wait, the more uncomfortable most people become. By interacting immediately, you show you are confident and want to talk. Plus, it casts you as a powerful "person of influence" who helps others make connections.

Many new employees avoid joining ongoing conversations at work because they feel that they may be intruding or that their coworkers are "cliquish." Here again you can show your confidence and professionalism by encouraging newcomers to join your group.

First, send out friendly signals using body language. Make eye contact, smile, keep your arms unfolded and angle your body outward toward the person who you think wants to join you. Next, create an opening in the circle of your group where the new person can easily enter and comfortably stand. You can even offer a friendly wave or nod that says, "Come join us." When the person joins you, be sure to introduce him or her to the others in the group.

S = SHAKE HANDS

Shaking hands is an ancient ritual dating back to Roman times. In those days, shaking hands showed that neither person held a weapon. Today, it is a ritual business greeting, but more important, a firm handshake between men and women signals mutual respect, confidence and professionalism.

However, there is still confusion about who should first extend a hand, the man or the woman. I can already hear those people quoting Emily Post's rule: "Men should wait for the woman to offer her hand first." Yes, that was the proper thing to do *fifty years ago*, but not today, especially in the business world.

To add to the confusion, many women wait for the man to make the first move. If neither man nor woman offers to shake hands, both feel uncomfortable. Therefore, I recommend that men and women offer to shake hands with anyone they meet in social and business situations.

E = EYE CONTACT

Steady eye contact shows interest, encourages others to talk and, most important, shows you are listening. Avoiding eye contact, looking away or closing your eyes for a few seconds creates a negative impression.

For some people, eye contact is the most difficult body language skill to master. If you feel uncomfortable with eye contact, these tips can help:

- Eye contact does not need to be an unbroken pupil-to-pupil connection. Look at the person's entire face as you talk and listen.

- Occasionally your gaze may focus elsewhere as you chat. After a moment, return your gaze to the eyes and smile.

- Don't fix your gaze only upon one person as you chat within a small group. Be sure to establish eye contact with everyone participating in the conversation.

When you communicate with *P-O-I-S-E*—Position yourself, Open stance, Interact immediately, Shake hands and Eye contact—people will feel more comfortable talking to you. In addition, adopting a confident posture can actually make you feel more self-assured.

Now you are ready to send consistent messages with your verbal and nonverbal language. But what messages can you send that make others like you and respect you?

Four Ways to Make Your Coworkers Like and Respect You

"Being popular is important. Otherwise, people might not like you."
—Mimi Pond, American writer

Although Hollywood film producer Louis B. Mayer was not particularly well liked by his peers, hundreds of people attended his funeral. His equally unpopular partner, Samuel Goldwyn, explained the huge turnout: "The reason so many people showed up at his funeral was because they wanted to make sure he was dead."

Everybody wants peer respect, but how do you get it? Dale Carnegie, author of *How to Win Friends and Influence People*, suggested, "Make people feel good about themselves and they will feel good about you."

Earning the respect of your coworkers is not like winning a popularity contest. Lasting respect among your peers is built and maintained by competently and fairly doing your job. Use the following tips, and your coworkers will like and respect you.

- Treat everyone with equal respect.

- Be competent, not conceited.

- Find out what people do well and praise them.

- Take a personal interest in others.

"The lame tongue gets nothing."

—Proverb

To communicate effectively, speak clearly and eliminate feeble phrases, jargon and verbal ticks from your vocabulary. Expanding your vocabulary and using poised body language will project power, confidence and competence.

CHAPTER TWO

Building and Managing a Winning Team at Work

"You can observe a lot just by watching."

—Yogi Berra, New York Yankees catcher and coach, 1925–

In this chapter, you will learn:
• **Three kinds of interview questions to ask potential team members** • **Three questions to ask when you delegate tasks** • **Four more feedback techniques that increase motivation and improve results** • **Twenty ways to be a more charismatic team leader**

During his first term as president, Dwight D. Eisenhower appointed Arthur Burns chairman of the Council of Economic Advisors. In their first meeting, they agreed to use memos to communicate with each other. Eisenhower said, "Arthur, keep it short. I can't read." Burns replied, "Mr. President, we'll get along fine. I can't write."

Three Kinds of Interview Questions to Ask Potential Team Members

"Never hire someone who knows less than you do about what he or she is hired to do."

—Malcolm Forbes, American publisher, 1919–1990

Finding the right people for your team can be a daunting task. What are your team's needs? Where will the recruits come from? What are their needs and skills? Will the new people get along with the veterans? How long will you need to hold their hands until they can function independently? Will they blend in easily with the way your team works, or will personality clashes derail your best-laid plans?

Learning answers to these questions before a worker joins your team may not be possible, but you can learn a lot about a job candidate's working style by asking the following types of questions.

QUESTION TYPE 1: Problem-solving questions

You can ask problem-solving questions based on real-life or hypothetical situations to discover how a potential team member

- Approaches problems

- Thinks under pressure

- Listens for details

- Asks for clarification

- Gathers data

- Processes information

- Develops problem-solving strategies

Here are a few examples of problem-solving or scenario-based questions that you can prepare before an interview.

"This is the problem, and here are the facts. What strategies for solving it do you suggest?"

"Here's the situation: Your supervisor is unavailable, and the client tells you he wants a decision right now. What would you do?"

"How would you handle an emergency such as . . . ?"

"How would you deal with a coworker who . . . ?"

QUESTION TYPE 2: Behavior-based questions

Behavior-based questions allow a person to describe how he or she has dealt with challenges and goals in specific situations. Knowledge of past behavior will help you determine how the person will act when similar situations arise in the future. By asking behavior-based questions, you can learn about his or her

- On-the-job training and experiences

- Mastered skills

- Personality traits

- Successes and failures

- Understanding of industry issues

- Level of professionalism

Here are a few examples of behavior-based questions:

"Tell me about a time when you had to handle an angry client or coworker."

"Describe a situation where you had to solve a problem at work."

"Describe how you handled a decision by your supervisor that you did not agree with."

"Tell me how you handled a major setback in a project."

"Give me a specific example of how you coped with a difficult problem under pressure."

QUESTION TYPE 3: Work-style questions

You know that personality clashes and conflicting working styles can quickly undermine the morale and effectiveness of your team. Questions about a potential team member's individual working style provide you with an insight into his or her weaknesses and strengths when working with others.

These questions help you determine if an individual is compatible with your management style and your team's way of working. Larger teams often break into smaller groups or pairs, so team members need to get along. By asking work-style questions, you can learn about a potential team member's

- Preference for working in large and/or small groups
- Style of interacting with managers
- Preference for formal or informal communication
- Choices for partners
- Ability to prioritize jobs
- Willingness to ask for help

Here are some examples of work-style questions:

"Do you prefer to work alone, one-on-one or in groups?"

"What type of people do you enjoy working with most?"

"Do you like formal or informal working relationships?"

Now that you have your team together, your next challenge is to prioritize and delegate tasks.

Three Questions to Ask When You Delegate Tasks

To effectively delegate, ask your team members the following questions:

1. "Will this new task prevent you from finishing your other assignments on time?"

If the answer is yes, then it is up to you to either give the person more time or help to complete the assignments. Piling one job on top of another without making the needed adjustments will only create tension and animosity among your staff.

2. "Do you have any questions about what I want you to do and when the job needs to be finished?"

Clearly defining your objectives and timetable will get concrete results. When delegating tasks, provide some examples or specifications for what you want. Be sure to follow up with, "Does what I've asked you to do make sense?" and "Is this timetable reasonable given your other responsibilities?"

3. "What do you need to complete this assignment? Is there anything else you need from me to get this done on time?"

Make sure your colleagues have the necessary tools, resources and time to accomplish their tasks. Otherwise, the chances are slim that they will finish the work correctly and on schedule. Remember to also include a few words of appreciation. For example, you can say, "Thanks. I really appreciate you taking on this assignment."

Now that your team is working up to speed, you'll need to keep them motivated and fine-tune their efforts. Do you know how to use praise to accomplish both these tasks?

Four Feedback Techniques That Increase Motivation and Improve Results

"I love criticism as long as it's unqualified praise."
      —Noel Coward, British actor and playwright, 1899–1973

I recently asked a production manager why he only criticized his staff's work. He responded, "I was trained to find mistakes, so that is what I focus on and look for."

I then asked, "But what about all the things your staff does right? Don't those things deserve to be mentioned, too?" He responded, "Not really. They're expected to get it right. That's their job!"

Getting it right is what most competent workers strive for and what managers expect, but compliments on a job well done are always appreciated. Use the following feedback techniques, and you will see better results.

FEEDBACK TECHNIQUE #1: Be specific about what worked

Saying "Good work!" is not enough. Zero in on the exact task and follow up with, "I especially like the way you . . . I think it will solve the problem we had with the. . . ."

FEEDBACK TECHNIQUE #2: Ask, "How did you do it?"

This management technique asks for the person receiving positive feedback to identify the steps and articulate the procedures that got the desired results. By doing so, he or she gets to shine a bit. In addition, both of you can identify aspects of the process that worked and can be used again. You can say:

"Please tell me what you did to get these results."

After the explanation, say something like:

"I want you to keep doing what you are doing."

If other workers can benefit from the procedure, say:

"I'd like you to show your method to Diane and Bill and see if it helps them, too."

FEEDBACK TECHNIQUE #3: Offer specific criticism without being harsh

As with positive feedback, the key to offering constructive criticism is being specific. However, because most people are sensitive to criticism, be tactful with your comments. Base any criticism you have on established criteria or objectives, and never make demeaning personal attacks.

Here are some tactful ways to say that you are *not* satisfied with an outcome:

WORDS THAT DON'T WIN	WORDS THAT WIN
"This is all wrong."	"This still needs work."
"You always have to do things your own way."	"I thought we had agreed that. . . ."
"Are you deaf?"	"Please listen carefully."
"You aren't up to this job."	"I think you need some help with this job."
"I should have done it myself."	"This is how I would do it."

Never make vague remarks such as:

"I don't know—I just don't like it."

"I'll know it when I see it."

"This is terrible!"

FEEDBACK TECHNIQUE #4: Ask the person to explain his or her approach and discuss where it failed to yield the desired results

"It's clear that we've got a mistake somewhere. Tell me what you did so we can find the problem."

Listen carefully for problems such as:

- Insufficient instructions
- False assumptions
- Misunderstandings
- Missing or incorrect information
- Insufficient training

- Lack of support

- Broken equipment

Then say:

"After what you've told me, it seems to me that you need to. . . . What do you think?"

Also, be ready to take responsibility for any errors or omissions on *your* part. You can say:

"Now that you've explained what you did, I think I see the problem. Sorry, it was my mistake. I was wrong to assume that you knew about. . . ."

"I see now that you didn't have the right information. That was my mistake. Next time I'll make sure you have everything you need before I assign you a job."

CONTINUOUS IMPROVEMENT COMES FROM CONSTRUCTIVE FEEDBACK

By initiating a "continuous improvement" approach with your team in a project, they will have the opportunity to work out bugs and avoid potential problems. Of course, problems at work always come up, but by using this constructive approach to giving criticism and feedback, you will get better results from your team.

You now know what it takes to build and maintain a smooth-operating team. But what can you do to instill loyalty, provide leadership and increase your charisma?

Twenty Ways to Be a More Charismatic Team Leader

"The old believe everything; the middle-aged suspect everything; and the young know everything."

—Oscar Wilde, Irish-born British playwright, 1854–1900

Managing Across the Generations

Bruce Tulgan, author of *Managing Generation X: How to Bring Out the Best in Young Talent,* advises business leaders all over the world on how employees from different generations can work together more effectively.

Tulgan cites today's fast-paced, rapidly changing workplace as a major source of conflict between younger and older workers. "The older the worker," he says, "the less likely he or she is to like the change. The younger the worker, the more likely he or she is to embrace the changes and want to accelerate them."

What does Tulgan say to older workers who consider young managers as too inexperienced to lead projects? "Today, what matters most is not always how much a manager knows, but how quickly he or she can learn and delegate. What may be most valuable in a leader is not always experience, but rather ambition, sense of urgency and speed."

How about younger workers who think their older team members are too set in their ways? To this Tulgan says, "The one thing which you cannot accelerate on the learning curve is wisdom. Older workers have watched new initiates succeed and fail. They have seen a lot, done a lot and they know a lot."

Finally, the most important thing different generations can do to improve their teamwork? Bruce Tulgan says, "Without a doubt, take the time to listen and learn from one another."

There is an old military joke about how Admiral Chester Nimitz and General Douglas MacArthur are clinging to scraps of wreckage floating in the middle of the ocean. Nimitz confesses, "It's a good thing my men can't see me like this—I can't swim." Not to be outdone, MacArthur says, "It's a good thing my men can't see me. I can't walk on water."

Do you know how certain dynamic people can just walk into a meeting room and all heads turn to take notice? These successful leaders exude confidence, style, charm and charisma—those mysterious forces who captivate and attract others. Famous business people, actors, models, politicians and athletes are not the only ones who are charismatic—you can be, too. Here are some ways to be a more charismatic team leader:

1. Tell your team members about your vision or goals.

2. Exude optimism and be willing to face critics and pessimists with a smile.

3. Consistently demonstrate your conviction with effort.

4. Build support for your ideas by encouraging others to personally identify with your purpose.

5. Distill your ideas or concepts into a simple and memorable message.

6. Convey the essence of your ideas in a "big picture."

7. Motivate others by showing them the benefits of their working with you.

8. Be animated and use plenty of gestures as you speak.

9. Infuse your stories with dramatic words.

10. Modulate your voice so it ranges from intimately soft to strong. Know the right time and situation for each.

11. Laugh at other people's stories and jokes.

12. Do a good job, but do not take yourself too seriously.

13. Express confidence through the tone of your voice and your body language.

14. Move through a crowd with the purpose of meeting and getting to know as many people as possible.

15. Volunteer to speak at an upcoming meeting or event.

16. Let others know that you empathize with their causes and goals.

17. Take a leadership position and get others to feel emotionally involved in your ideas and goals.

18. Lead a group discussion when the opportunity arises.

19. When you are the center of attention, enjoy it.

20. Take risks and do things that have a positive impact on people's lives.

"If you wish to know a man (or woman) give him (or her) authority."

—*Proverb*

Building and managing a winning team at work takes planning, clearly defined objectives and smart hiring. Once your team is in place, continue to motivate, improve and fine-tune your group. Now you know what it takes to be a leader. Your staff will respect and follow you when you show them you believe in them and in yourself.

CHAPTER THREE

Managing Staff Conflicts
Like a Diplomat

"Diplomacy is the art of letting someone else have your way."
—Daniele Vare, Italian diplomat, 1880–1956

In this chapter, you will learn:
- Three fast ways to cool yourself down in a heated conversation • Ten things you can say and do to stop feuding coworkers • Eight steps to defuse an angry subordinate • Four tips that wipe the slate clean and boost staff morale

President Abraham Lincoln listened as Edwin Stanton, his secretary of war, read aloud an angry letter peppered with curse words and insults that he had written to a troublesome general. After Stanton finished the letter, Lincoln applauded the powerful language, but then said, "You don't want to send that letter. Put it in the stove. That's what I do when I have written a letter while I'm angry. It's a good letter, and you had a good time writing it and feel better. Now burn it, and write another."

Like Secretary Stanton, managers today have to be aware of the words they use with subordinates. Even the most experienced supervisors admit that much of their time on the job is devoted to dealing with "people problems."

When you are a manager, effectively handling staff situations increases your credibility. However, if you ignore staff conflicts, everyone in your group will suffer.

Three Fast Ways to Cool Yourself Down in a Heated Conversation

"A lot of people look up to Billy Martin. That's because he just knocked them down."

—Jim Bouton, Yankees pitcher

Between the years 1975 and 1988, baseball manager Billy Martin was hired and fired five times by Yankee owner George Steinbrenner. Known for his hot temper and on-field antics, Martin would yell and kick dirt at umpires and even get into fights with his players. Although he was often difficult to work with, Billy Martin is still considered one of baseball's all-time great managers.

Some talented workers can be hard to handle. When that happens, keep your cool. Use these three stress-reducing techniques to remain poised and calm when you are in tense face-to-face discussions with a member of your team.

1. TAKE A FEW DEEP BREATHS. BE SILENT FOR TEN SECONDS

Deep breathing helps relieve stress, while remaining silent can keep you from saying something you might later regret. Use this time to consider your choice of words and imagine how the other person will react. If you foresee a negative response, keep quiet until you can come up with words you think will get a better reaction.

2. CALL A "TIME OUT"

Before you and the other person reach the breaking point, briefly withdraw from the heated conversation. Taking a short walk can prevent saying words in anger that both of you will later regret. Calmly suggest, "I think we both need a short break. Let's take five minutes and cool off." Then walk away, but be sure to come back.

3. TELL YOURSELF, "BE COOL AND STAY CALM"

When you are in a tense discussion, do you tell yourself, "I'm going to say the wrong thing"? If your inner voice bombards you with this negative "self-talk," you will begin to believe what you hear. To stay cool, replace this self-talk with a simple, positive message. The next time you find yourself engaged in a heated conversation with a staff member, silently repeat to yourself, "Be cool, stay calm. I can handle this." You will be surprised how effectively these words can help you keep your emotions in check so the verbal skirmish does not escalate into a major battle.

Ten Things You Can Say and Do to Stop Feuding Coworkers

"If you cannot answer a man's argument, all is not lost; you can still call him vile names."

—Elbert Hubbard, American publisher and author, 1856–1915

Shouting matches at the copy machine and arguments during staff meetings cause tension among coworkers, but only if you let them continue. Feuding coworkers create a hostile work environment for everyone, and it is the manager's job to end the dispute. Here are tips for calling a truce and mediating a resolution. You must be firm and not appear to take sides.

I. SPEAK WITH AUTHORITY AND DO NOT TAKE SIDES

Say: "I'm not taking sides or blaming either of you."

2. BE FIRM AND DIRECT. TELL THEM TO STOP.

Say: "I want you to end your feuding now, because when you are arguing, you're not working. I'm sure you'll never be best friends and you don't even need to like each other, but you need to get along if you want to continue working here."

3. TELL THEM HOW THEIR BEHAVIOR AFFECTS OTHERS. SAY THAT YOU ARE NOT GOING TO PUT UP WITH IT

Say: "When you two argue in staff meetings it wastes everyone else's time, too. I'm not going to let that continue to happen."

4. CITE SPECIFIC BEHAVIOR THAT YOU WANT TO STOP

Say: "I'm not going to tolerate any more abusive language, shouting, arguing or ridiculing each other's opinions in staff meetings."

5. OFFER OTHER WAYS FOR THEM TO EXPRESS THEIR VIEWS

Say: "If you disagree with something the other person says, put it in writing, give it to me and I'll be the judge."

6. EMPHASIZE THAT YOU ARE SERIOUS AND HAVE THE SUPPORT OF YOUR EMPLOYER OR BOSS

Say: "Our company policy is clear. It does not tolerate verbal abuse, making threats or creating a hostile work environment. I'm telling you right now that if both of you don't cool it, I'll have to write a memo that will go into your personnel files."

7. ASK BOTH PEOPLE TO WORK TOWARD A COMPROMISE

Say: "I am willing to mediate a solution to your disagreement, but only if you both are willing to compromise."

8. IF POSSIBLE, MINIMIZE THEIR CONTACT

Say: "As a 'cooling off' measure, I'm assigning you to different areas."

9. ARRANGE A THREE-WAY MEETING

Say: "You have a few days to think about what I've said. Then I want to meet with you both at the same time and discuss the dispute. The goal of the meeting will be to promote a better working relationship."

10. ASK BOTH PEOPLE TO AGREE TO A TRUCE

Say: "Before you go back to work I want to know right now: Are you willing to call a truce?"

If the feuding pair refuses to call it quits, then consult with your human resources department, company policy or supervisor before taking any further action.

Ending a feud may not be easy, but everyone you work with will benefit. In addition, your efforts send a signal to the rest of your group that interpersonal conflicts have no place on your team.

Eight Steps to Defuse an Angry Subordinate

"Anger restrained is wisdom gained."

—Proverb

Austrian born Rudolf Bing (1902–1997) loved the twenty-two years he spent as the general manager of New York's Metropolitan Opera. However, he hated the hysteria, shouting and confrontations that surrounded labor negotiations with the opera's trade unions. During one heated bargaining session, Bing leaned across the table and said to one boisterous union member, "I'm awfully sorry, I didn't get that. Would you mind screaming it again?"

Some angry subordinates swear, complain loudly, pound their desks or threaten to quit. Other, less obviously disgruntled workers sulk, do substandard work, make snide remarks or give you the "cold shoulder." When you see a pattern of angry behavior, it is time to act. The more you interact with your staff, the sooner you can spot any signs of "bad behavior." According to the *Journal of Management,* workers often express anger with these actions:

- Arguing with coworkers

- Emotional outbursts

- Frequent interruptions

- Frequent lateness or absenteeism
- Rough or inappropriate physical contact
- Withholding information
- Slow cooperation
- Spreading false rumors
- Dirty looks
- Condescending or sarcastic remarks

Psychologists blame increased anger in the workplace on heavier workloads, frequent layoffs, shorter deadlines, cramped office space, a sour economy and the list goes on. Whatever the reasons for the conflict, most agree that the sooner you defuse a subordinate's anger, the better. What can you say or do to defuse an angry subordinate? Experts in conflict resolution, mediation and conflict prevention suggest taking the following steps:

STEP 1. Show concern

Say: "There is something I'd like to ask you. Can I talk to you in private for a minute?"

Showing a disgruntled worker that you want to find out why he or she is angry helps in three ways. First, it demonstrates your concern for his or her feelings. Second, talking builds rapport and trust—two essential ingredients to resolve and prevent conflicts. Third, it sends the message that you want the angry behavior to stop.

STEP 2. Open the discussion

Say: "You seem angry or upset about something. What's wrong? Whatever you tell me is confidential."

Do not expect an angry person to be completely open or honest with you. He or she may be afraid of offending you or saying something that can be used against him or her.

STEP 3. Encourage the angry person to speak

Say: "I know this might be hard for you to talk about, but I'm willing to listen and I want to help, if I can. So tell me, what's bothering you?"

If he or she still refuses to talk, back off and say, "Okay, think about it for a day or so. The sooner you talk about why you are angry, the sooner we can do something about it."

STEP 4. Use active listening when the angry person finally speaks

Say: "What you're saying is that you feel. . . . Is that right?"

Paraphrasing the angry worker's statement shows that you have listened carefully. It helps the other person know that you understand there is a problem and hopefully, feel less angry. Acknowledging his feelings is often the most important step to resolving the problem. Once your subordinate does open up, actively listen for his feelings, facts and implied meanings. Also, pay close attention to your subordinate's body language and tone of voice. Both can reveal feelings that the person is too embarrassed or reluctant to express.

STEP 5. Seek clarification

Ask: "What do you mean when you say . . . ?" or "Why was that a problem?"

A less-outspoken subordinate may hesitate and talk around the subject until she trusts you enough to say what's really on her mind. Be prepared to hear criticism of you or other staff, but do not argue or defend. To show you are receptive and listening, remain quiet and maintain open body language—steady eye contact, arms unfolded and hands away from your face.

STEP 6. Apologize when it is appropriate

Say: "I'm sorry that something I said made you feel that way. I assure you I never meant to hurt your feelings." or "I apologize for. . . ."

A simple apology can do wonders, especially for ordinarily content workers. For example, several years ago I was working as a senior editor at a major publishing company. Five minutes into a discussion at an editorial meeting, my boss shouted at me, "Shut up!"

After his outburst, I said nothing for the rest of the meeting. I was angry and embarrassed that he talked to me that way. After the meeting ended he caught up with me in the hall and said, "Don, sorry about that. I was out of line in there. It's just been one of those mornings." I was surprised how quickly I felt my anger subside at his apology. I said, "Apology accepted. I hope your day improves."

STEP 7. Show a willingness to help

Ask: "What can I do to make you happier here?"

Once the person has opened up, continue the mediation process by finding out what he or she really wants. Asking is usually the fastest way to elicit this information. Listen for something that you can agree on. Say:

"I agree that you deserve a day off to compensate for all the overtime you have put in."

Acting on a valid grievance is the best way to discharge a disgruntled employee's anger. However, *never* make promises that you cannot keep or do not have the authority to grant. What can you do if you do not agree with the angry subordinate's solution or you do not have the authority to do anything about the problem?

If you disagree or you are not sure how to respond, paraphrase the person's view and take some extra time to think of a satisfactory response. Say:

"Am I correct in saying that you want . . . ? Let me think about what you've said, talk to my boss and then get back to you in a day or two. We'll can talk more about it then."

If you cannot do anything or choose not to grant the person's request, offer an alternative solution and a willingness to discuss it further. Say:

"I've thought over what you told me and discussed it with my boss. I have to deny your request for a . . . because. . . . However, I am willing to. . . . You may not feel that this is an ideal solution, but that's the best I can do for you right now. If you have another idea on how to deal with this problem, tell me. I'm willing to discuss it. I want you to be happy here."

STEP 8. Ask for something in return

Say: "Now I'd like you to do something for me. Tell me the next time something happens here at work that upsets you so we can work it out *before* it causes a bigger problem."

If the person still seems angry or resistant to your request, do not pressure him or her for an immediate commitment. Say:

"Why don't you take some time to think about what we've discussed. Let's talk again in a few days and see how you feel."

Make sure to follow up, showing the person you are committed to finding a solution.

Four Tips That Wipe the Slate Clean and Boost Staff Morale

"Last week I saw my psychiatrist. I told him, 'Doc, I keep thinking I'm a dog.' He told me to get off his couch."
—Rodney Dangerfield, American comedian, 1921–

Rodney Dangerfield has performed thousands of jokes that make himself the object of ridicule. He quips, "I don't get no respect. I worked in a pet store and people kept asking me how big I'd get."

However, getting "no respect" at work is no laughing matter. Low morale, staff arguments, reprimands, poor performance reviews and lay-offs—one or more of these can make people on your team feel depressed. However, if you let their motivation continue to spiral downward, you could be in for even more conflict! Here are some ways to boost your team's morale and inspire them to be productive again.

TIP #1: Mend fences

By accepting responsibility for your mistakes and forgiving a team member for his errors, you are on the way to a better relationship. Say:

> "I think both of us could have handled the situation better, but it's history now. I'd like to put it behind us and go on to our next project. How about you?"

TIP #2: Smooth ruffled feathers

Conflicts with staff can result in bruised egos. Before you can expect staff members to resume their usual levels of productivity, do some "stroking." Reassure them that you still appreciate their work and efforts. Say:

> "You know that I think you are really great at your job. Okay, we had a problem, but we worked it out. So let's move on. Now I want to change the subject. What new ideas do you have for our next program?"

TIP #3: Assign subordinates more tasks they like and fewer tasks they dislike

One way to improve morale is to have your team members focus their efforts doing the work-related tasks they are good at and enjoy. So before giving assignments, find out the tasks staffers prefer and those they dislike. Another way to accomplish the same goal is to encourage team members to trade away tasks they do not like, but only *with your approval*. Say:

> "I want you to check with me first, but if you can swap an assignment you don't like with a coworker for one that you prefer, go ahead."

TIP #4: Lighten up, smile, talk and be friendly

Conflict makes everyone on your team uptight, and if you remain angry or silent, your staff might feel like they have to walk on eggshells. Then more conflict is likely to erupt with the smallest provocation. Because your team looks to you for leadership, quickly reestablish a congenial atmosphere. Make an extra effort to be friendly and even a little playful. Offering everyone a smile and a few friendly words in a cheerful tone say that you are not upset with anyone and that you want to get back to business as usual. But you don't need to wait for a crisis to let your staff know that you care.

"Good words cool more than cold water."

—Proverb

The secret to managing a staff like a diplomat is to avoid common conflicts and to quickly smooth over ruffled feathers when they do arise. Knowing what *not* to say will also keep your staff happy. Your ability to defuse feuding coworkers or an angry subordinate will test your communications, but if you handle these tricky staff situations the right way, everyone's morale will improve.

CHAPTER FOUR

Getting Along with
Difficult Coworkers

"I'm not arguing with you—I'm telling you."
—James Whistler, American artist, 1834–1903

In this chapter, you will learn:
• **Three strategies that help resolve conflicts** • **How to say you disagree** • **How to avoid conflict with difficult coworkers** • **Seven tips to get along better with difficult coworkers** • **Ten polite ways to say "no" to difficult coworkers**

Conflicts between coworkers can begin with a simple disagreement or crass remark, turn into a nasty spat and escalate into emotional shouting matches—but only if the conflict is allowed to go that far.

If you handle a conflict before it turns into an all-out war, you can reach a successful resolution and avoid losing your cool—and possibly your job.

Three Strategies That Help Resolve Conflicts

"Quarrels would not last so long if the fault were only on one side."
—Duc de la Rochefoucauld, French writer, 1613–1680

Hollywood producers Samuel Goldwyn and Louis B. Mayer had a tempestuous partnership. They often argued and sometimes even came to blows. Once in the locker room of a Los Angeles country club, Mayer shoved Goldwyn into a laundry hamper. A witness to the altercation asked Mayer why he disliked his partner so much.

The movie mogul replied with astonishment, "What? We're like old friends. We're like brothers. We love each other. We'd do anything for each other. We'd even cut each other's throats for each other!"

Like Goldwyn and Mayer, many coworkers have disagreements. In fact, conflict is often part of working with other people. How you and your coworkers deal with differences can determine your success or failure in the workplace. Use the following strategies to help you keep conflict from ruining your working relationships.

STRATEGY #1: Suggest discussing the problem

When you approach your coworker, always keep your emotions and comments in check, no matter how much you want to rebuke your adversary. Although you are angry, stay calm, maintain eye contact and keep a neutral tone to your voice. Shouting or making a scene might make you feel better, but an angry exchange will only exacerbate the situation. You can take the initiative and say something like:

"We really need to discuss what's been going on between us here at work. Can we meet for a few minutes before lunch or after work to clear the air?"

"We clearly have a problem, but I think it is in both of our interests to resolve it. I'm willing to talk about it if you are."

Resolving a conflict is easier when both parties show a willingness to:

• Listen to each other without interrupting.

• Take each other's views into consideration.

• Make reasonable concessions and compromises.

• Avoid emotional outbursts and personal accusations.

Both you and your coworkers need to agree to these ground rules before you start your talk.

STRATEGY #2: Pinpoint the problem

Understanding the real problem—and not just from your own point of view, but from the other person's perspective, too—is essential in resolving a conflict. Ask yourself how you might have contributed to the disagreement. Sometimes a thoughtless act, sarcastic remark or poor decision can needlessly set off a conflict.

First, elicit your difficult coworker's perspective of the problem. Be sure just to listen without defending yourself or interrupting. For example, you can say:

"How do you see the problem we're having?"

"What is it that I'm doing that is causing you a problem?"

Responding to a criticism by saying, "*I see how that might cause* you *a problem.*" This acknowledges the other person's views and will go a long way to defusing a tense situation. After listening, you can say:

"What else?" or "Can you give me an example?"

These will encourage your colleague to be more specific and get to the heart of the problem. Keep in mind that some difficult coworkers will hesitate to say how they truly feel and what is bothering them. After they finish, then it is your turn to share your perspective of the problem. Be direct, but tactful. You can say something like:

"Here is how I see the problem."

"This is my view of the situation."

"You might not agree with me, but this is my opinion."

STRATEGY #3: Search for a workable solution

Your greatest chance to resolve a conflict with a difficult coworker is to find a mutually acceptable solution and agree to it. A difficult coworker might be more willing to accept a compromise if you ask for his or her solutions before you offer your own. For example, you might say:

"So how do you see us solving this problem?"

After he or she answers, do not respond right away. First listen and quietly consider what he or she says. Then say something like:

"Interesting. I'll think about what you've said."

"I think I can do that."

Ask for some clarification or offer your ideas for workable compromise. If you can tie your ideas together into one solution, your chances of reaching a working compromise increases. For example, say something like:

"I have an idea that might satisfy both of us."

"I can see how both of our ideas can work together."

Don't use heavy pressure to get a commitment or try to force your solutions on your colleague. Instead ask:

"Does that solve the problem from your perspective?"

"Is there anything you would add to that?"

Continue to discuss and define the solutions until you reach an agreement. Restate what you believe you have agreed to, then ask for a commitment.

"Okay, so as I understand it, we've agreed to . . . Is that right, and is it something you can live with?"

"Just so we're sure we understand one another, tell me what you think we've agreed to."

How to Say You Disagree

Coworkers do not always need to agree to resolve a conflict, since both might be right or wrong about how to handle an issue or how to determine the source of the conflict. Therefore, it is helpful if you:

- Listen to understand—not to convince.
- Identify assumptions that create misinterpretations.

To show that you are willing to accept a view that differs from yours, you can say:

"At least if we can't agree on . . . , perhaps we can agree to disagree with no hard feelings."

"I respect your views, but I disagree with them."

You will not be able to solve all of your conflicts, but these three strategies can help you defuse many problems with difficult coworkers before misunderstandings escalate into feuds. However, you can identify potential troublemakers and use specific strategies to stop some conflicts before they begin.

How to Avoid Conflict with Difficult Coworkers

President Lyndon B. Johnson was famous for withering remarks, especially when he could use them to intimidate a bureaucrat. One day, while walking past a paper shuffler at the Texas National Youth Administration, Johnson said loudly enough for everyone in the office to hear, "I hope your mind isn't as messy as that desk." The next morning, the embarrassed colleague had cleared his desktop of every paper. When Johnson strolled by, he remarked, "I hope your mind's not as empty as that desk."

Like most people, you probably have met your fair share of difficult people in your workplace. Because you might not be able to avoid these prickly coworkers, your next best alternative is to identify their foibles and to interact with them in a way that minimizes their negative impact.

Although the list of difficult coworkers is endless, here are the most common types and strategies for coping with their annoying behavior.

BLOCKERS

These aggressive coworkers stand in your way and oppose whatever it is that you want to do. They have their own agendas, ways of doing things and goals. Because they do not have the power to boss you around, their objective is to impede your progress.

Strategies for Handling Blockers
Do:
- Disagree with Blockers without arguing.

- Ask Blockers to keep their criticisms to themselves during brainstorming sessions.

- Challenge Blockers to add constructive suggestions to a previous idea.

Don't:
- Let Blockers put you on the defensive.

- Let Blockers dominate your discussion.

- Allow Blockers to stop your efforts.

What You Can Say to a Blocker
If a Blocker says, "That'll never work."

You can respond, "I disagree. I think it will work."

If a Blocker says, "That's the worst idea I've ever heard."

You can respond, "Do you have a better idea?"

If a Blocker says, "You'll be sorry if you do that."

You can respond, "I'm willing to take that risk."

COMPETITORS

To these aggressive coworkers, everything—from a simple conversation to a staff meeting—is a competition with a winner and loser. They love to taunt and tease the people they see as their opponents by attacking their credibility. Their primary objective is to dominate others and make sure that they come out on top.

Strategies for Handling Competitors

Do:

- Congratulate the Competitor when he or she succeeds.

- Suggest that you work together toward a mutual goal.

- Suggest competing in a sporting activity outside of work.

Don't:

- Accept a win-lose challenge from a Competitor at work.

- Play one-upsmanship with a Competitor.

- Brag to a Competitor when you achieve your goals.

What You Can Say to a Competitor

If the Competitor says, "Let's bet on who makes the most sales this month."

You can answer, "What's the point? We are on the same team."

If the Competitor says, "I'm definitely better at . . . than you are."

You can say, "Maybe you are. So what?"

If the Competitor says, "I'm sure our boss would rather have me handle the new account. I don't think you're ready yet."

You can reply, "I think that decision is up to our boss."

SABOTEURS

These devious coworkers undermine your projects, plans, meetings and goals behind your back. They might never openly oppose you, but they will scuttle your efforts every chance they get. They offer false information, spread rumors or belittle your results. Their objective is to prevent you from reaching your goals.

Strategies for Handling a Saboteur
Do:
- Approach Saboteurs carefully—they can be vindictive.

- Encourage Saboteurs to elaborate on a veiled criticism.

- Counter Saboteurs' rumors by explaining your side.

Don't:
- Confront Saboteurs in front of others.

- Expect much cooperation from Saboteurs, even when they say they are on your side.

- Let Saboteurs prevent you from achieving your goals.

What You Can Say to a Saboteur
If a Saboteur says, "I heard your project is in trouble."

You can reply, "Not so. Let me set the record straight."

If a Saboteur says, "Ah . . . great concept."

You can ask, "You don't sound very enthusiastic. What is it that you don't you like about my idea?"

If a Saboteur says, "Some people think your idea stinks."

You can reply, "Everyone is entitled to his or her opinion. What do you think?"

MANIPULATORS

Manipulators are passive-aggressive coworkers who use others to achieve their goals. They cozy up to and flatter coworkers to get them to do their work, then take the kudos for a job well done. Meanwhile, these sneaks avoid responsibility and blame others for their mistakes. Their objective is to get someone else to do their work.

Strategies for Handling a Manipulator
Do:
- Be polite and professional with Manipulators.

- Clearly define each of your responsibilities when you share assignments with a Manipulator.

- Remain vigilant. Manipulators are persistent.

Don't:
- Let Manipulators charm you into relationships they can use for their own benefit.

- Argue with Manipulators.

- Agree with Manipulators when they blame others for their mistakes.

What You Can Say to a Manipulator
If a Manipulator says, "You're so good at . . . , and I'm so hopeless. Do me a favor, will you, and handle it for me?"

You can respond, "Sorry, I'm on a deadline."

If a Manipulator says, "Don't you think Fran is out of her depth with this project?"

You can reply, "No. Actually, I think she's doing a good job, and I'm enjoying working with her."

If a Manipulator says, "This foul-up wasn't my fault—talk to Harry."

You can say, "No one's blaming you. Just fix it."

TIME BOMBS

Time bombs are those silent, sometimes volatile, passive-aggressive co-workers who act as if they might explode into a temper tantrum at any time. Their intimidating behavior causes you to limit your requests and "walk on eggshells" when they are around. Time bombs know that if they "go ballistic" a few times or even raise their voices, you won't ask them to do much. Their goal is to avoid work and responsibility by threatening a confrontation.

Strategies for Handling a Time Bomb

Do:

- Show a willingness to work together with a Time Bomb.

- Be patient, tactful and consistent with Time Bombs.

- Find a balance between flexibility and assertiveness.

Don't:

- Let Time Bombs intimidate you.

- Be overaccommodating or aggressive.

- Break any promises or make any decisions without first consulting them.

What You Can Say to a Time Bomb

If a Time Bomb says, "If I hear that one more time, I'm going to explode."

You can say, "You seem upset. What's wrong?"

If a Time Bomb says, "I'm so sick of this garbage."

You can ask, "Do you need some help?"

If a Time Bomb says, "Why don't you just lay off?"

You can reply, "Sorry, I didn't mean to upset you."

SOCIAL BUTTERFLIES

These passive-aggressive coworkers constantly chatter about how much they have to do, yet they rarely seem to be working. Instead, they talk nonstop with cubicle mates, chatter endlessly on the telephone and gossip at the water cooler and copier. They fritter away their own time, waste the time of coworkers and make it difficult for people working within earshot to concentrate. Their objective is to socialize, and as a result, their work goes undone.

Strategies for Handling a Social Butterfly
Do:
- Be friendly but limit the time you chat.

- Tell chatty coworkers to please hold down the noise.

- Cut off their attempts to gossip about others.

Don't:
- Let their talking with other coworkers continue to distract you from your work.

- Get angry when you ask them to keep their voices down.

- Chide them for not being busy (that's your boss's job).

What You Can Say to a Social Butterfly
If a Social Butterfly says, "Have you heard what I've been hearing about our new production manager? Whoa!"

You can reply, "Well, I've heard he's doing a great job and that department has really improved."

If a Social Butterfly says, "Remember Margie? Well, you won't believe what I just heard about her."

You can reply, "Sure, but, I'm really busy right now. By the way, I could really use some help."

If a Social Butterfly says, "I met this great-looking guy/gal last night at this club I go to. Anyway, to make a very long story short, we just started talking and. . . ."

You can say, "Sorry to interrupt, but I've got to get back to work. Maybe we can chat at the break or over lunch."

SLACKERS

These passive coworkers take pride in their low productivity. They usually dislike their jobs and just go through the motions without caring about the outcome. They offer no ideas, take no initiative and only produce the bare minimum. They have a seemingly endless supply of excuses for their poor performance. Their objective is to work as little as possible.

Strategies for Handling a Slacker
Do:
- Explain to a Slacker how his or her work affects you.

- Tell a Slacker that you are working on the same team.

- Say that their work matters.

Don't:
- Accept unsatisfactory work from a Slacker.

- Accept a Slacker's excuses for substandard work.

- Allow a Slacker's poor performance to reduce the quality of your efforts.

What You Can Say to a Slacker
If a Slacker says, "No one cares."

You can say, "I care."

If a Slacker says, "I'm doing the best I can—given this lousy equipment I have to work with."

You can say, "Maybe you can talk to our boss about getting a new computer or using another work station."

If the Slacker says, "Why should I bother?"

You can respond, "If we're going to work together, you're going to have to do better than that."

COMPLAINERS

Complainers are those passive coworkers who always moan and groan about what's wrong and why ideas will never work. They whine their way through the day to anyone who will listen to them. They waste your time with their whining, grumbling and criticizing—instead of pulling their weight and doing their share of the work! Complainers drag their coworkers down to a subsistence level of motivation, enthusiasm and productivity.

Strategies for Handling a Complainer
Do:
- Give Complainers some attention, because that is what they really want.

- Offer Complainers a suggestion or two (but don't be surprised if they don't follow your advice).

- Limit the amount of time you will listen to a Complainer.

Don't:
- Join Complainers in a gripe session.

- Get involved in a Complainer's dispute with another coworker.

- Ignore legitimate gripes or problems if you can do something about them.

What You Can Say to a Complainer

When a Complainer says, "This job sucks."

You can reply, "Have you ever considered transferring to another department?"

When a Complainer says, "I always get the worst jobs."

You can suggest, "I know . . . is looking for people with your skills, and they, I hear, have better benefits. Maybe it's time to move on."

When a Complainer says, "I hope I win the lottery so I never have to come back to this lousy place."

You can reply, "It's easier to find another job you like better."

You now know some ways to identify and some strategies for handling difficult coworkers. You can get along with these hard-to-handle people if you remember the old adage, "Honey catches more flies than vinegar."

Seven Tips to Get Along Better with Difficult Coworkers

"Flattery is like a cigarette—it's all right as long as you don't inhale."
—Adlai Stevenson, American political leader, 1900–1965

Surprisingly, you can head off major conflicts with difficult coworkers with a few kind words and actions. Try a few of these tips and just watch the positive impact they have on cantankerous colleagues.

Tip #1: Show appreciation for a difficult coworker's effort on your behalf.

Tip #2: Do something nice for your difficult coworker.

Tip #3: Offer a difficult coworker praise and recognition.

Tip #4: Give your difficult coworker a compliment.

Tip #5: Chat with a difficult coworker.

Tip #6: Ask a difficult coworker for opinion or advice.

Tip #7: Help out a difficult coworker in a crunch.

You can see that dealing with difficult coworkers takes patience, tolerance and some cleverness, too. However, even with all these tips and strategies at your disposal, there will be times when you still need to say this important word: "No."

Ten Polite Ways to Say "No" in Difficult Situations

"You know she speaks eighteen languages. And she can't say no in any of them."

—Dorothy Parker, American wit, 1893–1967

Two colleagues were debating the value of being polite with their coworkers. "Everyone knows that being polite is nothing but hot air," one fellow sneered. "Ah, there's nothing but air in a tire," his colleague responded, "but it makes riding in a car very smooth and pleasant."

Do demanding coworkers make your day miserable with one request after another? There comes a time when you need to stand firm and deny their requests. Here are ten typical requests and the ways to politely say "no" loud and clear.

- If someone asks you to contribute to another office gift fund, you can say something like:

    "No, I'm going to give a gift on my own."

- If a coworker asks you for a loan until payday, you can say something like:

    "My heart says yes, but my bankbook says no, no, no."

- If a colleague asks you to work late, you can say:

    "Sorry, I'm busy tonight. Maybe Jenny can help you out."

- If a coworker asks you to tell the boss a "little white lie," you can say something like:

  "That's a very bad idea. The answer is no."

- If a coworker asks you to vouch for his or her attendance at an offsite meeting or event, you can say:

  "No way. Are you crazy or trying to get us fired? That would be a big mistake for both of us. The answer is no."

- If a person on your team asks you to complain to your boss about another coworker, you might say:

  "No, I don't have a problem with him and don't want to take sides. You'll need to work out the problem between the two of you or ask our boss to mediate."

- If a coworker pressures you to organize an office party, you can something like:

  "No, I'm sorry but I can't. I'm just too busy."

- If an office colleague asks you out on a date and you don't want to accept, you can say:

  "I appreciate the invitation, but no thanks."

- If someone at work asks you to hire a friend for a job instead of a more qualified applicant, you can say:

  "No, that would be unethical."

- If a coworker asks you to help out with a project that you don't have time for, you can say something like:

  "Sorry, I can't help. Maybe you can ask the boss for some extra help."

Denying a coworker's unreasonable request might not always be easy, but use the examples in this chapter to stand your ground—and be polite and assertive. Remember that you have the right to say "no."

It's not only what you say, it's how you say it."

—*Proverb*

Handling conflict with difficult coworkers is a challenge, but spotting the signs of a conflict and using the right strategies can help. Remember that *how* you disagree or say "no" can help avoid conflicts, especially with difficult people. Now that you know how to talk and resolve issues in small groups, it's time to get on stage and talk to larger audiences.

CHAPTER FIVE

Mastering the Art
of Public Speaking

"An after-dinner speech should be like a lady's dress—long enough to cover the subject and short enough to be interesting."

—R. A. Butler, British statesman, 1902–1982

In this chapter, you will learn:
• **Six key questions to answer before you speak** • **How to structure your presentation with a beginning, middle and end** • **A three-point stance for impromptu presentations** • **Cures for the five most common presentation problems**

President Ronald Reagan was a masterful public speaker, especially when simplifing complex issues for the American people. For example, during his first televised budget speech, he showed a handful of coins to illustrate the current value of the dollar. Even his Democratic rivals marveled at his skill. One admitted, "It takes an actor to do that. Carter would have emphasized the wrong words. Ford would have fumbled and dropped the cash. Nixon would have pocketed it."

Are you passing up career opportunities because you feel uncomfortable speaking before an audience? Do you break out into a cold sweat if your boss asks you to "say a few words" during a department meeting or sales presentation? Does your brain freeze or your tongue twist like a pretzel when you have to think on your feet? If you have answered yes to any of these questions, you are not alone. Even pros get nervous before they speak to audiences.

Whether you lack confidence or experience, you can talk with confidence when you use the following public speaking techniques.

Six Key Questions to Answer Before You Speak

"A speech that does not strike oil in ten minutes should stop boring."
—Louis Nizer, American attorney, 1902–1994

Unless you are a confident impromptu speaker, do not wait until you are in front of the audience to decide what to say. This casual attitude can lead to a rambling, irrelevant or embarrassing presentation. By answering the following six questions, you can make your presentations more focused, audience-oriented and successful. Plus, you will be a more confident and professional-sounding speaker.

1. What is the purpose of your presentation?

2. What is the title or theme of your talk?

3. Who are the people in your audience, and what do they know about your subject?

4. How will the audience benefit from your talk?

5. What main points do you want to cover?

6. What do you want the audience to do after you finish?

Once you have answered these six questions, you are ready to create your presentation, complete with a beginning, middle and end.

How to Structure Your Presentation with a Beginning, Middle and End

"Begin at the beginning and go on till you come to the end; then stop."
—Lewis Carroll, British writer, 1832–1898

Think of all the stories, movies, television programs, songs and even speeches you have heard. They all have one thing in common—a beginning, middle and end. When you plan a presentation and provide an introduction or beginning, a middle that presents your information, and an end that sums up everything you have presented, your audience will hang on your every word.

THE BEGINNING: GRAB YOUR AUDIENCE'S ATTENTION

How can you grab your audience's attention in the first few moments of your speech? There are many ways to begin a presentation. You can use one of the following "grabbers" to hook your audience and keep them listening.

- Ask a short-answer or "yes or no" question.

In my networking workshops I begin by asking:

> "Have you ever walked in to a room full of strangers at a convention and felt nervous or uncomfortable? If your answer is yes, please raise your hand."

Asking your audience an easy-to-answer question grabs their attention and prepares them for what you are about to say. By asking the audience to "raise their hands," you will immediately connect with them and see who is listening.

- Cite a dramatic statistic or quote a respected source about a surprising trend.

For an audience of tough-minded executives or business owners, offering hard, cold facts might be a good way to grab their attention. For example a presentation on customer retention might begin with:

> "According to a recent article in the *Harvard Business Review*, more than half of the top sales reps who left their jobs took the company's best customers with them to their next position."

When you quote a source, be sure your facts and numbers are correct and that you can back them up. Nothing undercuts your credibility or confidence faster than being caught fudging your statistics or being unable to identify your sources upon request.

• Share a personal experience or story.

Opening your presentation with a personal or dramatic story is an excellent way to grab the audience's attention. For example, one man in my public speaking workshop started a presentation to a national sales conference like this:

> "I was never so scared in my whole life. The plane vibrated like a jalopy as it climbed up through the clouds. I clenched my teeth, hoping that would keep my kneecaps from knocking. The wind howled through the open hatch so loudly that I barely heard my instructor ask me, 'Are you ready?' Before I had time to answer, he shouted, 'Jump!' Now I'm asking all of you sitting before me, 'Are you ready to jump into a new a new sales program?' Before you answer, jump!"

• Tie your introduction to the purpose of your talk.

Hooking your introduction to the purpose of your presentation serves as a bridge to the middle section. For example, a first-aid instructor begins his talk with a dramatic statistic about heart attacks and then says,

> "The purpose of my talk today is to show you an incredible life-saving technique anyone can learn: cardiopulmonary resuscitation, commonly known as CPR."

THE MIDDLE: FILL IT WITH PLENTY OF "MEAT AND POTATOES"

Devote most of your presentation time to the middle section, and be sure to include plenty of solid information. Presenting solid information does not mean your talk needs to be dull. As you prepare your talk, think of it as a good meal. Your presentation needs something an audience can sink their teeth into that also tastes good.

For example, the meat and potatoes of a status report might consist of three main points: last month's sales figures, current sales and goals. To spice up your report, support each main point with a short example that gives your audience the "story behind the numbers." To spice up your talk even more, add a quote or short, humorous anecdote that reinforces a main point.

THE END: MAKE YOUR CONCLUSION MEMORABLE

Ending your presentation with a memorable conclusion helps people remember you and what you have said. Follow these three steps and end your presentations with a bang.

- Step 1: Summarize your key points.

  For example, "In the last few minutes, you've heard three examples of how our department is getting closer to our quarterly quotas."

- Step 2: Ask your audience to do something.

  For example, "Now, I'd like you to . . ."

- Step 3: Close with a bang.

End with a short, well-rehearsed story, appropriate joke, or quote that sums up what you've said. Be sure to thank your audience for their attention. For example:

> "In closing, I'd like to leave you with these few words by. . . . *(Be sure to memorize or read your quote)*. Ladies and gentlemen, thank you for listening!"

A well-prepared presentation boosts your credibility and inspires your audience's confidence. But what can you do if you only have a few minutes to prepare your talk?

How You Talk to Yourself Matters

Peak performance specialist Dr. Dan Schaefer, Ph.D., is a psychologist and hypnotherapist who helps business people, professional athletes, Olympic contenders, academics and artists overcome personal barriers to winning and success.

To his clients—several of whom are Fortune 100 CEOs and top sales executives—Schaefer says, "How you talk to yourself is as important for succeeding in business as it is in winning a sporting event. Pay close attention to your self-talk. Notice it. Decontaminate it. Turn it down or off."

How can you use this self-talk strategy when you are preparing for a presentation? Dr. Schaefer suggests that you ask yourself these questions:

"What do you hear yourself say to yourself?"

"What begins your negative self-talk, and how long does it last?"

"When does negative self-talk end, and how do you stop it?"

Dr. Schaefer advises you to replace any negative self-talk with a positive script. Repeat to yourself *everything* you want to happen—exactly the way you want it to happen—from the beginning to the end of the conversation. He says, "The conscious mind acts out its most dominant thought."

Does that mean you should say to yourself, I think I can. I think I can. I think I can, just like the main character in the children's book *The Little Engine That Could?*

According to Dr. Schaefer the answer is, "Yes."

A Three-Point Stance for Impromptu Presentations

"Spontaneous speeches are seldom worth the paper they are written on."
—Leslie Henson, actor and comedian, 1891–1957

Do your legs turn to jelly if someone says, "We'd like you to say a few words at our meeting" and you're given little or no time to prepare?

If your answer is "yes," do not panic. You can impress your audience if you use a three-point stance for impromptu presentations.

POINT #1: State your main point or purpose

Get right to the point in one topic sentence. Say:

> "I'm going to tell you about the rate increases and changes in our company's insurance benefits program and what you can do about it."

POINT #2: Tell the most convincing evidence or example

Use the most compelling facts and examples to support your main point or views. For example:

> "An independent audit completed last month found that these increases are necessary because of a 10% increase in overall medical costs."

POINT #3: Tell your audience what you want them to do or conclude from your comments

State your conclusion right after you have offered supporting evidence. For example:

> "Therefore, if you sign up with the updated plan, your new copayment will be increased by 10%, but your benefits will increase."

President Franklin D. Roosevelt might have offered the best advice for mastering impromptu talks: "Be sincere. Be brief. Be seated." However, when you do speak, make sure that your voice commands the audience's attention.

Cures for the Five Most Common Presentation Problems

"They were really tough—they used to tie their tomatoes on the end of a yo-yo, so they could hit you twice."

—Bob Hope, American comedian and actor, 1904–

Even experienced speakers know that eventually a presentation—for one reason or another—will not go as planned. There might be a person who interrupts or heckles you, a squealing microphone or faulty equipment. These are just a few of the things that can disrupt your presentation.

Speaking pros also know that when things go wrong on stage, they can lose their train of thought, become tongue-tied, even lose their tempers. That is why they always prepare for what can go wrong. Here are some common problems that can derail your talk and ways to solve them.

PROBLEM #1: You forget what you are saying and you freeze

Your presentation is going great and everything is under control. Then something distracts you and—*wham!* First your brain freezes and then your tongue turns into an ice cube. As the seconds tick by, your brow beads with sweat. The longer you remain silent, the more paralyzed you become. Your audience senses your distress and shifts uneasily in their seats. What will you do next?

What *not* to do: Do not panic or bolt from the room.

What to do: Take a deep breath, drink some water, smile and look at your notes. Find the main point you were discussing and pick up where you left off. You can say, "So getting back to my main point, . . ."

If negative thoughts fill your mind, quickly replace them with confidence-boosting self-talk such as, *I can handle this. Be cool. I can continue.* In most cases, your audience will be rooting for your speedy recovery.

PROBLEM #2: Audience members chat during your talk

You are just getting into the meat and potatoes of your presentation as two people seated in the back row whisper and laugh loud enough for everyone to hear. They don't stop even after you given them your best "stop it" look. Do not let them continue to disrupt your presentation.

What *not* to do: Do not raise your voice, lose your temper or scold the offenders.

What to do: In a firm but friendly voice, say:

"Excuse me, you folks *(use their names, if possible)* in the back row. I need your attention up here." (For most people, this is enough to get them to stop talking.)

Another option: Put them in the spotlight. Say:

"Would either of you in the back row care to share your comments with the rest of us? Our time is limited, but if there something that you would like to quickly add to what I've said before we continue, go ahead."

This technique can embarrass the talkers into silence. However, be aware that this response might encourage the attention-seekers to spout off now that they have everyone's attention. If the talkers accept your offer, be prepared to quickly put an end to their comments by interrupting:

"Excuse me. Thanks for your comment, but now I want to pick up where I left off."

A more assertive option: The private chat.
If possible, give the rest of the group a short activity or break. Then go to the offending pair and in a polite, quiet and firm voice say:

"I've asked you twice to end your side conversations. You are making it difficult for people to listen. Do me a big favor—save your side conversations for the break. Otherwise, I'm going to ask you to leave."

PROBLEM #3: A heckler starts giving you a hard time

I once had a heckler in a conversation workshop who interrupted my opening comments with this jab: "How can you prove that?" I briefly answered him, and a minute later, as I suggested an easy way to break the ice, he sneered, "I tried that and it didn't work."

How do you stop a heckler before he makes you look like a fool or you lose your temper? First, realize that hecklers usually have three goals: 1) test your confidence; 2) undermine your credibility; and 3) show off.

What *not* to do: Do not over-react, ignore, get into a discussion with, defend yourself, lose your temper or—although it might be tempting—put down the heckler with a stinging one-liner.

What to do: Stay cool and keep your sense of humor. If possible, offer a quick answer or an example that supports your point. This might be enough to silence the heckler.

If the heckler continues and goes beyond what you consider acceptable behavior, call for a short break. Go up to the person and gently ask him or her to accompany you out of the room. Then privately suggest that he or she leave.

What can you do if the heckler is a coworker who is annoying you just for fun? You might not be able to ask him to leave the room, but you can approach him and quietly say in a pleasant but firm voice, "I'd really appreciate it if you would stop interrupting me."

The sooner you deal with a troublemaker, the better it is for you and your audience. After all, the speaker's first obligation is to the people in the room who came to listen.

PROBLEM #4: You are asked a difficult question that you cannot answer, or in the Q&A (question and answer) portion of your presentation, you face a roomful of silent faces

The Q&A portion of your program is a great opportunity to connect with your audience, so do not let it fall flat. An effective Q&A allows you to clarify information, emphasize main ideas, and listen to the views and concerns of your audience. Here are few ways to handle a question that you don't know the answer to. You can say:

"I don't know (or I don't have that information at my fingertips), but I'll see if I can find out for you."

"Your question is actually quite complex and one that really deserves more discussion than we have time for today. However, my short answer is. . . ."

Here's how you can avoid a silent Q&A session.

If someone asks you a question during the break say:

"That's a great question! Will you kick off the Q&A portion of my program with that question?"

Start your Q&A with, "Who has the first question?"

If no one speaks, have a kick-off question of your own to ask. For example:

"One question that I'm frequently asked is. . . ."

"Now you might be wondering, 'What's the next step?' Here's the answer."

PROBLEM #5: Your audio-visual equipment fails

What can you do if have an equipment failure at the precise moment you need it in your presentation? Make a few little jokes as you take *less than a minute* to reboot your computer, fiddle around with the on-off switch or change light bulbs (if you know how). If you want to use humor to handle the situation, you might say:

"I knew I should have bought the extended warranty."

"I don't understand. This worked last year."

If you want to remain serious, you can say:

"Please take this moment to discuss . . . with the person next to you."

Tips for a Better Q&A Session

- Anticipate questions and prepare short answers.
- Always repeat or paraphrase the question so everyone knows what was asked. (This gives you a few more seconds to compose a succinct answer.)
- Keep your answer short with concrete examples.
- If the question does not relate to the topic, say, "Good question, but it's outside the scope of today's topic. I'd be happy to talk to you about it afterward."
- Thank each person for his or her question and then ask, "Who has the next (or last) question?"

If you cannot solve the problem within a minute, call for an "A/V person"—if one is available—to help you. Then continue with your presentation. Have a back-up plan for the electronic presentation portion of your program, including visuals or charts in a handout. You can prevent (some) technological problems in the future if you:

- Check all equipment before the presentation begins.
- Reboot the laptop computer *after* you have tested your program.
- Have back-up disks, overheads or handouts.
- Make sure overhead transparencies are clean and appear in the correct order.
- Make sure slides are in the slide projector trays correctly.
- Learn to switch bulbs in an overhead projector.

Remain flexible because you might need to speak without your A/V. Use A/V to enhance, not carry, your program. Then, if your electronics fail, you can continue with your talk. I still keep old-fashioned (but reliable) flipcharts or white boards with new markers handy in case I need them.

"The voice is the best music."

—*Proverb*

Answering questions about your audience, creating a solid structure and plenty of practice are the keys to giving a well-received presentation. If you make a mistake or fumble a bit, don't worry—just quickly get back to what you were saying. Share what you know and have some fun and your audience will applaud both you and your speech.

CHAPTER SIX

Convincing Your Boss to Boost Your Career

"The world is divided into people who do things and people who get the credit."

—Dwight Morrow, American statesman, 1873–1931

In this chapter, you will learn:
• How to tune into your boss's conversational style • Blowing your own horn without sounding like a braggart • Two strategies to position yourself for a promotion • Dos and don'ts when asking for a promotion

Before Charles M. Schwab became the president of Bethlehem Steel, he learned a hard lesson about resting on your laurels from his employer, Andrew Carnegie. After boasting to his boss in a telegram: "All records broken yesterday." Carnegie wired him the following reply: "What have you done today?"

Tuning In to Your Boss's Conversational Style

"The bird is known by his note, the man by his words."

—Proverb

It's Monday morning, and the first thing you see on your desk is a note from your boss saying she wants to see you in her office—*ASAP!* You might not know what's on your boss's mind, but tuning in to her conversational style will help you climb the career ladder.

Bosses have many different conversational styles. Some like to chat before discussing work. Others prefer getting down to business right away. One boss might feel more comfortable talking one-on-one, slowly focusing on one detail at a time. Another might like to discuss ideas with a group around a conference table.

Observe your boss to determine which style of conversation he or she prefers. Of course, no one uses just one conversation style. Most people use a combination of styles, but one of the following four is probably most dominant.

- Forceful conversational style

- Friendly conversational style

- Coaching conversational style

- Logical conversational style

TALKING TO A BOSS WITH A FORCEFUL CONVERSATIONAL STYLE

"Strategic thinker," "mover and shaker," "hard-driving," "blunt"—these words all describe a boss with a forceful conversational style. As aggressive communicators, these people get to the point and frequently interrupt. Their loud voices and animated body language can be intimidating, especially when they express their views or give orders. They hate answers such as "No," "I'll try" or "It can't be done."

The boss with a forceful conversational style likes to discuss options, make decisions, then delegate the tasks and details to others. How do you deal with this communication style? In discussions, stand your ground, briefly present your case, but do not get into an argument, because these bosses usually insist on getting their way. A forceful boss wants results and then enjoys basking in the glory of success.

Your career can get a dramatic boost if you do not mind playing "second fiddle" to a boss with a forceful conversational style. Assure your boss that his or her objectives are your primary focus. All you have to say is, "Tell me what you need, and I'll take care of it." Here are six more tips to help you make a great impression on this kind of boss:

Dealing With a Forceful Boss Who Loses His Temper

Under pressure, a boss with a forceful conversational style might shout orders, make accusations or even threaten you. When that happens, avoid a direct confrontation, because you will always lose. You might cool your boss down with a few soothing words such as "It's going to be all right" or "No problem, I'll take care of it."

However, your best bet is to stay out of your irate boss's way by adopting a "duck and cover" approach until the storm blows over. If your boss pushes you close to your boiling point, you might need to say, "Please, I can't solve the problem when you are shouting at me."

- Skip small talk or personal inquires altogether or wait until after you discuss business. For example:

  "Good morning Ed. I'm all ready to go over our accounts for this month."

- Restate the main points to show you are listening and understand the "big picture." For example:

  "From what you said yesterday, I take it you are most concerned with. . . ."

- State the goal of your meeting in a sentence. Say:

  "In a nutshell, the purpose of our meeting today is to give you the story behind the numbers."

- Avoid long explanations or logical arguments. Say:

  "In a sentence, the answer to your question is. . . ."

- Leave details or background information for later. Say:

  "I won't go into the nuts and bolts now but ask if there are any details you want to know more about."

- Ask for advice on strategy, action or a decision on how to proceed. For example:

    "What would you suggest as a next step?"

TALKING TO A BOSS WITH A FRIENDLY CONVERSATIONAL STYLE

"Personable," "enthusiastic," "involved" and "upbeat" are words that describe the boss with a friendly conversational style. This engaging communicator is animated, likes small talk and shows a personal interest in coworkers. Bosses with a friendly conversational style encourage brainstorming and teamwork. They work hard to foster cooperation, harmony and productivity among their staff.

A boss with a friendly conversational style is not obsessed with details or upset by small mistakes. He or she focuses on the "big picture" by maintaining a balance between getting the work done to an acceptable standard and keeping coworkers reasonably happy. This kind of boss likes to laugh, joke and be the center of attention.

Developing a fun and productive working relationship is the right formula for impressing a boss with a friendly conversational style. You can speak up at meetings, offer ideas and be a team player. Tell your boss that you value your relationship, and he or she will go to bat for you when you want a promotion. All you have to say is, "I enjoy working with you" or "You make working here fun."

Here are more tips for talking to a boss with a friendly conversational style:

- Ask about your boss's family, hobbies and interests before discussing business. For example:

    "Before we get started on our budget, tell me quickly, how is your daughter feeling?"

- Be enthusiastic, especially during meetings and when receiving assignments. For example:

    "Pitching ideas to clients sounds like fun to me."

- Summarize your boss's main points. For example:

    "You want me to do . . . by tomorrow morning, right?"

Dealing with a Friendly Boss Who Ignores Problem Workers

A boss with a friendly conversational style might ignore a difficult worker instead of confronting him about the problem. When a boss lets a slacker get away with sub-standard work, for example, everyone else on the team suffers. As the problem grows worse, team morale and productivity quickly decline.

Although it might be inappropriate for you to chide a problem coworker, you can ask your boss to address the issue. Let your boss know how the person's behavior affects you and your coworkers, and ask him or her to act. You can say:

"I've got a problem that I'd like to talk to you about. Tina does a good job when she tries, but too many times her reports come to me with careless mistakes. I end up fixing her errors, in addition to preparing my own reports. I'd really appreciate it if you would talk to her about improving the quality of her work."

- Listen carefully and ask clarification questions. Say:

    "What exactly do you mean when you say the promo piece should 'knock their socks off'?"

- Be flexible and open to your boss's ideas. For example:

    "That idea of yours never occurred to me. I like it!"

- Avoid too many details or logical arguments. For example:

    "I won't bore you with details or long explanations. What's most important for you to know is. . . ."

- Say your main point in a sentence or two. For example:

    "Simply put, we need to make a buying decision by next Wednesday if we want to get the vendor's discount."

TALKING TO A BOSS WITH A COACHING CONVERSATIONAL STYLE

"Nurturing," "mentoring," "conscientious" and "teacher" describe a boss who favors the coaching style of conversation. These communicators take learning seriously and enjoy sharing knowledge. They value high-quality work, personal contacts and loyal relationships.

Bosses with a coaching conversational style ask questions to facilitate discussion at meetings. They delegate tasks, but only after providing their staff with the necessary information, specifications and schedules. Expect this boss to scrutinize your work and provide detailed feedback, not unlike a high school teacher.

Working independently to achieve high standards will turn a coaching boss into an advocate for your career advancement. Bosses who use the coaching conversational style value personal relationships, so be sure to show your appreciation for all efforts on your behalf. One easy way to do that is to say, "I appreciate your help."

Here are more tips for talking to a boss with a coaching conversational style:

- Show you want to always improve your performance. Say:

  "I'm attending a public speaking workshop because I want to be more effective in our staff meetings."

- Accept criticism gracefully. For example:

  "In what ways do you think I could do this better?"

- Seek clarification. For example:

  "What would you consider a job well done?"

- Speak up at meetings and offer ideas. For example:

  "I'd like to add something to what you've just said."

- Ask for your boss's opinions. For example:

  "In your opinion, what is the key issue?"

- Ask your boss for more responsibility. Say:

  "I'd like to work on . . . when you think I'm ready."

Dealing with a Coaching Boss Who Is Overbearing

Well-meaning bosses with a coaching conversational style can be overbearing. They press and cajole you to do it their way. If you disagree or do not follow their advice, these bosses might act aloof, defensive, patronizing, feel unappreciated or even get angry.

Of course, you want to take advantage of your boss's wisdom and experience, but at the same time reserve the right to make your own career decisions. To reduce tension in your relationship, do not overreact to your boss's criticisms or abundance of suggestions. Tell your boss that you appreciate him or her by saying:

> "I really appreciate all that you've done for me here at work. I might not have followed all your suggestions, but most of your advice has helped me a lot."

TALKING TO A BOSS WITH A LOGICAL CONVERSATIONAL STYLE

"Precise," "serious," "perfectionist" and "introverted" describe the boss with a logical conversational style. These reserved communicators present their ideas step by step, from beginning to end. Bosses with a logical conversational style love to discuss technical details, processes and how things work. Above all, they value accuracy and a systematic approach to everything.

Bosses with a logical conversational style avoid casual socializing with coworkers before meetings or on breaks. They often avoid small talk and usually prefer talking one-on-one about business-related problems and solutions or a high-interest topic.

You can win the support of this kind of boss by avoiding mistakes—both verbal and written. Choose your words carefully, speak slowly and take a methodical approach to your conversation. To show a boss with a logical conversational style that you strive for error-free work, say:

"I want this to be right, so tell me if there is anything that does not meet with your approval."

Dealing with a Logical Boss Who Becomes Hypercritical

Under pressure, a boss with a logical conversational style is less communicative but more critical than usual. When these bosses speak, they are blunt, impatient and intolerant of even the smallest mistakes, which they see as major failures. So do not be shocked if your boss spots a little goof in your work and snorts, "This is all wrong!"

Your best strategy for dealing with a hypercritical boss is to be fussy about even the smallest details. Do not bother arguing over the details or offering excuses because they will just antagonize your boss. When your boss criticizes your work, do not panic. Start taking notes and say:

"I see what you are saying. What else isn't right?"

Here are more tips for talking to a boss with a logical conversational style:

- Get to the point at the start of your meetings. Say:

  "Hi Jean. I'm ready to start going over the specs for the project."

- Check and recheck all details and supporting documentation before discussing your work. For example:

  "I've triple-checked our figures. Our department increased sales this month by 10 percent."

- Present detailed information sequentially from beginning to end. For example:

  "Here are all the details from start to finish. First, I began with. . . . Next I. . . . I continued with. . . . Finally, I finished with. . . ."

- Never offer excuses or an answer that you cannot back up with facts or examples. For example:

  "I don't know the answer to that question. I'll find the answer and get back to you."

Understanding your boss's conversational style makes it easier to know what to say and how to say it. The next step is to say how you have helped the company and your boss achieve their goals. The trick is to talk about your accomplishments, but not sound like you are bragging.

Tooting Your Own Horn Without Sounding Like a Braggart

"Don't talk about yourself; it will be done when you leave."
—Wilson Mizner, American playwright, 1876–1933

Heavyweight boxing champion Muhammad Ali elevated the art of self-promotion to a new level with his words, "I am the greatest!" A fellow boxer who grew tired of Ali's boasts asked him how he was at golf. "I'm the best," Ali grinned. "I just haven't played yet."

It is true that most successful people like to talk about their accomplishments. However, if you toot your own horn too loudly you will sound pompous and might blow your chances for advancement. If you want to impress your boss, avoid the following three mistakes when talking about yourself.

MISTAKE #1: Saying too much

It's okay to blow your own horn, but keep it short and sweet. In a sentence or two, describe specific actions you took that saved your boss time, the company money or improved customer satisfaction. For example:

  "The rep at ABC Stores told me that the products I sold them were moving like hotcakes."

  "I just ran the numbers. My idea for reordering supplies online will cut our office costs by 20 percent!"

MISTAKE #2: Exaggerating your accomplishments

Mark Twain once boasted to a fellow train passenger that he had caught dozens of trout on a fishing trip and that they were on ice in the baggage car. "You caught that many fish after the close of fishing season?" the man asked. "Very interesting! By the way, I'm the state game warden. Who are you?" Twain replied with a wink, "I'm the biggest damn liar in the United States."

You might be tempted to exaggerate sales figures, profits or positive customer responses when talking to your boss. However, this practice could put you and your boss in an embarrassing position if higher-ups ask you to back up your claim. Exaggerating your numbers might impress your boss in the short term, but eventually he or she will learn the facts. Then your credibility and chances for a promotion will go right out the window.

Instead of claiming bogus numbers, impress your boss with specific examples of how you turned a potential disaster into a success. For example, say:

> "It was a good thing I called the client to check on that delivery. They hadn't received it, so I called the warehouse and had them ship out another order."

> "The owner from Ace Trucks called about our invoice. But after I explained to him why we had to charge him extra, he said he'd pay the bill today."

MISTAKE #3: Failing to share the credit

Imagine a star athlete like basketball legend Michael Jordan taking all the credit for winning a game or league championship. What could be worse for player morale than listening to a braggart ignore the contributions of his or her teammates?

If you fail to share the credit for successes, the notes you blow on your horn will sound sour. When you take a cue from those gushing Oscar winners and spread the credit, your boss will see that you are a team player who deserves credit, too. Here are some ways to acknowledge coworkers.

"I couldn't have made the sale without the help of everyone in our department."

"Getting this contract was a team effort. I'm just the one who closed the deal."

Two Strategies to Position Yourself for a Promotion

"They needed a fiddle player and I got the job. They heard me play guitar a few nights later and gave me a job as a guitar player. You gotta be in the right place at the right time."

—Chet Atkins, American musician, 1924–2001

The 2000 college football season had just started, and second-string quarterback Ryan McCann sat on the UCLA bench. Less than ten minutes into the game with Alabama's Crimson Tide, UCLA's first-string quarterback injured his shoulder. Ryan McCann—untested but prepared to play—took over and lead the Bruins to three touchdown drives and a victory.

STRATEGY #1: Position yourself as a "second-string backup"

You can position yourself as a "second-string backup player," which means that you are ready to go to bat on a moment's notice. To play this role:

• Determine the skills of the "first-string" positions you want to back up.

• Assess your skill level, strengths and weaknesses.

• Upgrade your skills to the required level.

Tell your boss:

> "I've been upgrading my . . . skills, so if you need me to cover for . . . , I'm ready to step in."

> "Now that Lee is on extended leave, I'll do whatever you need to fill in."

> "Let me know if you need a volunteer to fill in for. . . ."

STRATEGY #2: Position yourself as a "resource"

Motivational speaker Anthony Robbins carved his niche in the training world by convincing people they could walk barefoot on a bed of hot coals without toasting their toes. Robbins now positions himself as a resource for Olympic athletes, CEOs and even U.S. presidents who want to achieve peak performance. Over the years, Tony Robbins has created a self-improvement empire based on this principle: "Every human is an invaluable irreplaceable resource."

You do not need to be as charismatic or successful as Tony Robbins to position yourself as a resource. All you need to do is help your boss improve profits and productivity, reduce costs or increase the company's competitive edge. You become a valuable resource by offering your boss the benefits of your skills, knowledge and professional contacts.

Here are other ways to position yourself as a resource:

- Refer other competent workers to your boss. Say:

  > "I know someone who would be perfect for the open position in our department."

- Get to know helpful people in your business. Say:

  > "I can recommend a designer (programmer, speech writer, etc.) who might be able to solve that problem for you."

- Help your boss stay abreast of industry trends. Say:

  > "I found this newspaper article about what we were discussing the other day. I hope it's helpful."

Four Things to Do Before You Ask for a Promotion

Preparation is a key to success when asking for a promotion. Be sure you have all your supporting documents and that you do your homework before meeting with your boss.

1. Prepare a one-page bulleted summary of your contributions to your department and company to increase its profits, efficiency and competitiveness.
2. Learn about the job you seek. Be ready to explain to your boss why you are a good candidate for the position.
3. Know what the position pays before you ask for a promotion. Be ready to suggest other forms of compensation that you are willing to accept.
4. Choose the right time to ask for a promotion. Hold off if your industry, employer or boss is struggling to stay afloat.

• Attend vendor-sponsored workshops, forums and conventions. Say:

"I met a vendor who might be able to give us a good price on that project."

• Discuss and compare notes with your boss about the industry trends and changing opportunities. Say:

"I read in several trade publications that by this time next year, a new software program called . . . is going to be standard in our industry."

The key to positioning yourself for a promotion is to be in the right place at the right time with the right skills. Of course, when an opportunity to climb the career ladder comes knocking, it is critical to know what and what *not* to say.

Dos and Don'ts When Asking for a Promotion

"Be nice to people on your way up because you'll meet them on your way down."

—Jimmy Durante, American comedian, 1893–1980

Knowing what (and what not) to say improves your chance of getting a promotion. Get right to the point, keep your "horn-blowing" brief and do not forget the most important thing—*ask for the promotion.*

PRACTICE BEFORE YOU ASK

Your goal is to make a smooth and confident five-minute sales presentation—and the product is *you*. List the key points you want to make on an index card and practice saying them into a tape recorder or video camera, to a trusted friend or a communications trainer.

How do you sound? Is your voice steady? Do your words communicate the main points? How do you look? Is your body language projecting confidence?

Remember to take into account your boss's conversational style when you ask for a promotion. Here are some dos and don'ts when asking your boss for a promotion:

Do say: "I'd like to talk with you for a few minutes about future career opportunities in this department." (This direct statement demonstrates initiative and spotlights your goal to move up the career ladder.)

Don't say: "You're too busy to talk to me about a job move." (This comment lacks confidence and sounds manipulative.)

Do say: "I've been upgrading my skills so when there is an opening, I'd like to be considered for the position." (This assertive comment says that you want a shot at the job.)

Don't say: "I'm tired of being passed over for promotions." (Whiny comments only make you sound bitter and incompetent.)

Do say: "Let me know when and where I am needed." (This offer suggests that you are the kind of person who is capable and willing to take on responsibility.)

Don't say: "I'm willing to do whatever it takes." (Although this comment implies that you are hard-working, it also implies that your ethics might take a backseat to results.)

Do say: "Can you tell me about any upcoming career opportunities that you think I might be suited for—even those positions that would require me to upgrade some of my skills?" (This question sends a confident message that you want your boss's help in moving up the career ladder.)

Yes, part of getting a promotion is being in the right place at the right time, but knowing what and what not to say to your boss can make a big difference, too. Don't be shy about blowing your own horn, but if you are not sure if something is appropriate to say to your boss, follow this sage advice: "When in doubt—leave it out."

CHAPTER SEVEN

How to Win Debates Without Making Enemies

"I love debate. I don't expect anyone just to sit here and agree with me, that's not their job."

—Margaret Thatcher, former British prime minister, 1925–

In this chapter, you will learn:
• **How to present a persuasive argument** • **Easy ways to make facts and statistics more convincing** • **Three rules of engagement for tactful debates with colleagues** • **Five strategies to punch holes in an opposing argument** • **Five ways to stay calm when someone challenges your opinion** • **Eight mistakes to avoid when disagreeing with a colleague**

I recently met an editor who told me how her company decides which books to publish. She explained, "Senior editors take turns debating for and against book proposals in front of five executive editors, the VP of sales and the publisher." She complained, "I'm afraid I haven't been very convincing. What am I doing wrong?"

Everyone has lost a debate at work over a project or proposal but do you know why your opponent won? Maybe she was more knowledgeable than you about the subject or could think more quickly on her feet. How do you outwit these silver-tongued adversaries? Ask successful lawyers, salespeople or negotiators and they will tell you that there are specific strategies for making a persuasive argument. You can win a debate using the following tactics:

- Take a stand.

- Offer convincing evidence to support your position.

- Scrutinize your opponent's facts and conclusions.

- Stay calm as you defend your views.

- Restate your opinion with conviction.

How to Present a Persuasive Argument

"You raise your voice when you should reinforce your argument."
—Dr. Samuel Johnson, British lexicographer, 1709–1784

A few years back I worked with a teacher in British Columbia who loved to debate other teachers about "open classrooms," "new math" and the "back-to-basics" movements in education. I observed that after their lively exchanges in the lunchroom, his opponents frequently adopted his point of view. When I asked my coworker his secret to winning these debates, he offered me the following advice.

I. TAKE A STAND

Are you for or against the proposal? Is it a good or bad idea? Do you believe the proposed solution is the right or wrong approach to the problem? What is your position?

To win a debate, you must take a stand and defend a definite position. When stating your point of view, consider your audience. Understanding their values and sensitivities helps you build persuasive arguments and avoid inflammatory remarks. To make it clear that you are taking a stand, preface your views with phrases such as:

"In my opinion, . . ."

"My position on the matter is. . . ."

"I am absolutely convinced that. . . ."

"It is my firm belief that. . . ."

2. SUPPORT YOUR POINT OF VIEW WITH CONVINCING EVIDENCE

If you want to persuade others and win debates, you will need to offer facts, examples and expert opinions that lead to your conclusion. Build support for your views with the following kinds of information:

Appeal to tradition

People like things that are safe and familiar. That's why wrapping your point of view with the mantle of tradition makes your job easier and your opponent's more difficult.

Let's say, for example, that you think your company should sponsor a money-raising event for a local cultural institution. You can say:

"ABC Company has a long history of improving the quality of life in our community. It has raised money for the new library and the park playground, just to name a few projects that we can be proud of. So I propose that we continue this tradition with a fund-raising dinner to help raise money for a new museum."

State facts and figures

The most effective way to build a case is with hard, cold facts. Who? What? Where? When? How many? How much? When you present facts and figures, be sure they are:

- Up-to-date and accurate.

- From a reliable and respected source.

- Simply stated and easy to understand.

Cite recognized authorities in the field

Using expert opinions can also help you present evidence that will help you succeed in winning your debate. Try to find a variety of authorities whose ideas support your views. In addition to aligning your views with those of experts, be sure to establish that each expert has:

Easy Ways to Make Facts and Statistics More Convincing

The America mystery writer Rex Stout (1886–1975) said it best: "There are two kinds of statistics, the kind you look up and the kind you make up." Even so, you will win more debates if you present numbers, facts and statistical evidence in a way that makes them more meaningful.

- Use large numbers. They impress more than small numbers, percentages or fractions. You can say something like this:

    "In a survey of more than 10,000 college graduates, nearly 7,300 of these job-seekers stated. . . ."

- Follow percentages with gross dollar figures when referring to money or profits.

    "An increase of 10 percent sales per week translates to a $50,000 increase in profits."

- Create a "bandwagon effect" by showing that a majority supports your point of view.

    "Nearly 900 of the 1,000 people who visited our website said they found our information helpful."

- Your audience's or opponent's respect.

- A record of predicting or achieving results.

- A track record on the topic under discussion.

You can say:

"Please don't just take my word for it. My proposal includes the opinion of Dr. Alice Edgar, a respected attorney with a Ph.D. in business from the Harvard Business School and a frequent contributor to the *Harvard Business Review*. Her opinion is. . . ."

Describe a similar situation

Successful attorneys and salespeople know they can use similar situations, or precedents, to present convincing evidence and bolster their arguments or convince clients. The key is to choose the right example that appeals to your audience and supports your point of view.

For example, let's say you want to alert a client to a potential problem that might come up six months down the road. You believe: "Forewarned is forearmed."

Your coworker disagrees with you and argues that it is better to wait until the problem actually occurs before telling the client, because it might never happen. He believes: "Don't make waves if you don't have to."

To use a precedent to win this debate, say:

> "A similar situation came up last year when I was working on another account. Here's what we did."

Appeal to higher moral values

Appealing to a higher moral value is most effective when you pit cold facts against human consequences. Sure, some heartless opponents might shrug their shoulders with indifference, but you might be able to embarrass or chide them into accepting your views by saying:

> "Yes, profits matter, but I believe we have an obligation to ensure the safety of our company's employees, even if it means cutting our profits. I think we need to do the right thing, don't you?"

3. STATE YOUR CONCLUSION WITH CONFIDENCE

How you present your conclusion can tip the audience's opinion in your favor. To win the debate, state your conclusion unequivocally. Then seek an agreement from your audience or opponent. Use the following phrases to signal that you are about to conclude and that your point of view is the correct one:

> "It's clear that the right decision is. . . ."

> "There's absolutely no question that. . . ."

> "I'm sure that you'll agree with me that. . . ."

Presenting a clear point of view, strong evidence and a firm conclusion are the first three steps to winning a debate. However, if you want to persuade your audience, you'll also need to probe your opponent's position for weaknesses without being arrogant or overbearing.

Five Strategies to Punch Holes in an Opposing Argument

"Nixon is the kind of politician who would cut down a redwood tree and then mount the stump to make a speech for conservation."
—Adlai Stevenson, American statesman, 1900–1965

In 1960, most experts predicted that Richard Nixon would soundly defeat the lesser-known John F. Kennedy in the upcoming presidential election. However, Kennedy believed he could persuade voters that he was the best candidate, but only if he did well on the nation's first televised debate.

Millions of television viewers tuned in to witness a poised and persuasive Kennedy repeatedly attack Nixon's weakest arguments. By contrast, Nixon looked stiff—some say even untrustworthy—as he gave uninspired answers. The day after the first debate, an elderly woman said to Nixon, "That's alright, Mr. Nixon. Kennedy beat you last night, but you'll win next time."

She was wrong. Kennedy won all four debates and the election because he used the following debate strategies.

STRATEGY I: Identify weak points and minimize strong points

Listen carefully to pinpoint the weakest points in the other person's position. Then focus on these areas by raising questions about them. Meanwhile, minimize your colleague's strong points to decrease their impact. Say:

"Your recommendations would improve the design *(strong point)*, but it's too expensive to make the changes because we've already started construction *(weak point)*."

Three Rules of Engagement for Tactful Debates with Colleagues

"My advice was delicately poised between the cliché and the indiscretion."
—Robert Runcie, British archbishop, 1921–2000

Yes, you want to win your debates, but not by humiliating your colleague. When the discussion is over, you might still need the other person's cooperation. Here are three rules of engagement for more tactful face-to-face encounters.

Rule #1: Never make personal attacks.

There are three reasons to never make a personal attack. First, personal attacks—claiming your colleague is dishonest, incompetent or insincere—implies that you have a weak argument. Second, personal attacks make you appear desperate because they frequently are a tactic of last resort. Finally, personal attacks turn friendly competitors into bitter rivals.

Rule #2: Never label your colleague.

Although labeling (or mislabeling) an opponent might be an effective strategy in political contests, it can easily backfire at work. Everyone has prejudices and viewpoints, and it's fair to highlight these differences for the sake of winning an argument. However, labeling your colleague—calling him sexist, for example—will only reflect poorly on you.

Rule #3: Never distort your colleague's position.

Your credibility is at stake when you debate an issue with a colleague. Don't misrepresent his or her position. It only hurts your credibility and can make you an enemy.

"I agree with you that we need to increase production *(strong point)*, but your solution to hire temporary workers will cause more problems later *(weak point)*."

STRATEGY 2: Challenge the sources and interpretation of the facts

During a presentation or debate, it can be difficult to tell real facts from manufactured ones. So questioning the use or accuracy of the other person's facts greatly improves your chances of winning. Here are several ways to decrease the impact of facts in an argument:

- Say that the facts are open to interpretation. For example:

    "I interpret the report quite differently than you do."

    "I question if these numbers support that decision."

- Say that the facts as presented lead to a false impression. For example:

    "Your facts only show a part of the whole picture."

- Question the validity of the facts—are they outdated or incorrect? For example:

    "How old is your data? If it isn't current, I question how useful it is to our situation today."

- Say that the facts are biased. For example:

    "If these numbers only come from one industry source, how can we be sure that they aren't biased?"

- Say that a crucial fact has been omitted. Say:

    "If an equal number of men and women did not take part in the study, how can you say that it is accurate?"

Keep in mind that if you dispute or question your opponent's facts or conclusions, be well prepared to offer information of your own that backs up your point of view.

STRATEGY 3: Challenge arguments based on popular appeal

You can undercut an argument based on popular appeal by comparing it to a higher moral or scientific standard. For example, you can say:

> "But popular positions aren't always the right positions. Remember that prior to the passing of the 1964 Civil Rights act, most Americans accepted segregation in our public schools as a fact of life. That was popular opinion, but that didn't make it right."

STRATEGY 4: Question the relevance of an example

Never let your opponent get away with citing an example that does not closely fit the situation under discussion. Here are three ways to say that a cited example does not apply to an argument:

- Claim that the example or situation is not similar enough to the case at hand, so it proves nothing. For example:

    > "The situation you just described happened under completely different circumstances. I don't see how it applies to the problem we are discussing now."

- Offer an example that more closely reinforces your point of view. You can say:

    > "I don't agree that the business model that worked in the 1980s is going to work today. Let me give you a different example of how we dealt with a situation much more like the one we are facing today."

STRATEGY 5: Suggest that your colleague has reached a hasty conclusion based on a faulty assumption

Implying your opponent based his or her conclusion on faulty logic can deliver the knockout punch you need to win a debate. However, never say "You're wrong!" Instead say:

"You've based your estimate on the assumption that we are going to sell more units this year than we did last year. What if our sales go down instead of up?

If you want to win arguments, you will need to do more than challenge facts and conclusions. You will also need to stay poised when someone challenges your arguments.

Five Ways to Stay Calm When Someone Challenges Your Opinion

"I am firm; you are obstinate; he is pig-headed."
—Bertrand Russell, British philosopher and social reformer, 1872–1970

There might be times during a debate when someone challenges your facts, accuses you of being wrong or even questions your competence. Perhaps he is desperately testing your confidence, trying to sidetrack your arguments or hoping you will lose control. Whatever unflattering comments your opponent makes, take a deep breath and keep your cool. Focus on making a response without including remarks that you may later regret. Here is what you can do and say to remained poised and confident when someone challenges you:

1. KNOW YOUR ARGUMENT'S WEAK SPOTS

Anticipate and prepare for the challenges against your position. Say:

"That question doesn't surprise me, since people who don't understand the nature of the problem assume that it is a crucial point."

2. DO NOT PANIC IF YOU LOSE A POINT OR GOOF

If your colleague points out a contradiction in your argument. You can say:

"Your point is well taken, but in the grand scheme of things, it has little bearing on the outcome."

3. DON'T BE RUSHED INTO A HASTY RESPONSE

Take your time and calmly respond to each challenge point by point. Repeat the question to give yourself a few more seconds to consider an answer:

"I'd like to answer your questions and concerns one at a time."

4. DON'T OVERREACT

Never react to outrageous remarks, charges or other taunts designed to make you lose your temper. Say:

"It seems to me that you don't have anything constructive to add to our discussion."

5. MINIMIZE YOUR OPPONENT'S CHALLENGES

Gloss over your opponent's attacks and repeat your conclusion. Say:

"Nothing that you've said changes the facts."

Staying calm when someone challenges you shows that you are confident enough to think on your feet without getting rattled. By keeping your emotions in check, you will win more debates without making the kinds of mistakes that turn opponents into enemies.

Eight Mistakes to Avoid When Disagreeing with a Colleague

"If I've done anything I'm sorry for, I'm willing to be forgiven."
—Edward N. Westcott, American writer, 1846–1898

When you disagree with a colleague's idea or approach to a project, there is more at stake than just winning and losing a debate. Your relationship and your job might also be on the line. Here are eight mistakes to avoid when you debate with your colleagues:

1. Ridiculing, embarrassing or humiliating your colleague in front of other coworkers.

2. Bringing up past errors or oversights.

3. Saying, "You're dead wrong!"

4. Repeating a negative remark made by someone else.

5. Implying that your colleague's views are not relevant.

6. Turning a business debate into a personal battle.

7. Ending the discussion with unfriendly or angry words.

8. Staying angry with a coworker after the debate ends.

"Speak well of your friends; of your enemy say nothing."

—Proverb

Disagreeing with a colleague can cause friction if you forget to be tactful. Even if you know you are right, if you want to remain on good terms, it is best to present your views as opinions, not facts.

CHAPTER EIGHT

Negotiation Strategies That Lead to Job Offers

"They say hard work never hurt anybody, but I figure why take the chance."

—Ronald Reagan, fortieth U.S. president, 1911–

In this chapter, you will learn:
• **Three critical questions to answer that improve your bargaining position** • **Five tips for negotiating a higher salary** • **Seven big mistakes people make during job negotiations** • **How to use silence and stalling to negotiate better offers**

Film producer Samuel Goldwyn was known as a tough negotiator, especially with employee salaries. When one actor told him how much he wanted per week, Goldwyn yelled, "You're not asking for fifteen hundred a week," he stormed. "You're asking for twelve, and I'm giving you a thousand!"

Once you've gone through the preliminary interviews, the next task is to negotiate the best possible job offer. Negotiating a job offer is a lot like other kinds of bargaining. It requires offers and counteroffers, give and take, effective listening and speaking skills, and of course, careful preparation. How do you prepare? The first step is to ask *yourself* the right questions before you sit down at the negotiating table.

Three Critical Questions to Answer That Improve Your Bargaining Position

"If you ask me anything I don't know, I'm not going to answer."
—Yogi Berra, Yankees manager, 1925–

Several years ago I was one of the final candidates for a senior editor position at a small publishing house. I met with the vice president to discuss the position. After chatting a few minutes about the company and job responsibilities, I asked how much the job paid. The man smiled and said, "I never discuss money on the first date."

That response set the tone for the entire job negotiation. It also taught me that I needed to ask more than just "How much?" if I wanted a good job offer.

Here are three essential questions to ask yourself that will improve your bargaining position.

QUESTION #1: Ask yourself, "What is my salary range?"

Determine the lowest amount you'll accept as well as the salary you want. These figures give you bargaining room so you and your prospective employer can agree on a combination of money and perks that you can both live with.

When it comes to discussing money, always hold out for more than you think you're worth. Or, to put a little twist on the words of business guru Harvey Mackay: "It's not how much you are worth. It's how much people think you're worth."

When the interviewer says, "The job pays . . . ," look a little disappointed. Then confidently smile and respond, "My salary range is. . . ."

If the interviewer answers, "That's not possible," say:

"I don't want to get hung up on salary before we discuss the all the issues."

QUESTION #2: Ask yourself, "What offer do I want?"

If you go into a job negotiation without carefully considering beforehand what you want in an offer, you are selling yourself short. Think about the job's salary range, compensation package, responsibilities and future opportunities. Identify exactly what you want when you negotiate a job offer.

In addition to discussing money, be sure to include all the concerns and interests you want to bring up in your negotiations. Some of your other concerns might include:

- Benefits
- Bonuses
- Future opportunities
- Housing allowance
- Office space
- Performance appraisals
- Raises
- Responsibilities
- Retirement funds
- Severance packages
- Sick days
- Support staff
- Teamwork styles
- Training
- Travel requirements and allowances
- Vacation
- Work hours

When you begin job negotiations, bring up these important concerns. After all, how can your prospective employer make you a great job offer, if he or she doesn't know what's important to you? For example, you can say:

"In addition to salary, I'd also like to discuss other issues that are important to me, such as. . . ."

QUESTION #3: Ask yourself, "What is my *walk-away* option?"

What will you do if you do not get the kind job offer you want? Are you stuck in the take-it-or-leave-it position, or can you end the negotiation because you have another—hopefully better—option elsewhere? Because every negotiation has several possible outcomes—not all of which are in your best interest—it is wise to know what the Harvard Negotiation

> ### Identify your strengths for negotiations before you start. For example, you are:
>
> - Well organized
> - Experienced
> - A self-starter
> - Self-directed
> - A strong finisher
> - Deadline oriented
> - A team player
> - Results driven
> - Efficient
> - Easy to work with

Project describes as your "B-A-T-N-A" (Best Alternative to a Negotiated Agreement). I call it the "walk-away" option. Here are some *B-A-T-N-As*:

- Stay in your current position until another job possibility comes along.

- See if you can negotiate a better deal at your present job.

- Continue looking for a job with competitors.

- Start your own business as an entrepreneur.

The stronger your walk-away option, the better your negotiating position with a prospective employer and the less likely you will be to get pressured into taking a job that you might later regret.

Five Tips for Negotiating a Higher Salary

"Money is better than poverty, if only for financial reasons."
—Woody Allen, American writer and comedian, 1935–

A young man and an older woman are negotiating a job offer. "Young man," said the woman. "I've interviewed a dozen applicants for this position, but I've chosen you. Consider it a clear vote of my confidence that you will do a great job. In answer to your request for more money, I've decided to increase my original offer by 10 percent." The fellow leaned back in his chair and sighed, "Thanks, Mom."

Even if your prospective employer is not a relative, you can still negotiate for a higher salary. Here are several tips to help you get the money you want.

TIP #1: Seek agreement that you are the best person suited for the job

Ask, "Have you found a candidate who is better suited than I am for this position?"

If the interviewer says, "No, but we are still talking to a couple people about the position," respond:

"I don't know about the other people you've interviewed, but from what you've told me about the job, I think I'm perfect for the position."

TIP #2: Discuss the job responsibilities in detail and ask the employer to agree to an expanded job descriptions

Ask, "Now that we have talked about the position in greater detail, would you agree that there are considerably more responsibilities involved than we had originally discussed?"

If the interviewer says, "Not really. All of our job descriptions are general and usually include additional responsibilities," you can say:

"My point exactly! That's why I strongly feel that the salary should accurately reflect the amount of work and responsibility involved, don't you?"

TIP #3: Show documents that highlight past accomplishments, including samples, testimonial letters, company newsletters, awards, etc. to prove you are worth more money

Say, "As you can see from these letters and documents, I frequently exceed sales quotas."

If the interviewer says, "These look great, but how do I know these are an accurate representation of all your work?" you can suggest:

"I'd want to know the same thing. Why not give my reference a call and ask her opinion of my work? Do you want her telephone number or e-mail address?"

TIP #4: Ask the employer to describe specific problems in the company and then tell how you would use your array of skills to solve them

Say, "According to what you've told me, I see several areas where I can help you. Here is how I would handle the production-inventory-distribution problems that you described to me a few minutes ago."

If the interviewer says, "That sounds good in theory, but how likely is it to work?" you can say:

"I handled a similar problem on my last job and my solution worked great. Based on what you've told me, I think I'd get about the same results for you here."

TIP #5: Seek agreement that you are worth more money

Ask, "You originally said that the job pays . . . , but if I can achieve better results than you expect, would you agree that I am worth paying a higher salary?"

If the interviewer says, "No. When we hire someone we expect great results all the time," respond with:

"Your standards are high, as are mine. Don't you think my salary should be commensurate with my results?"

Your prospective employer will probably try to get you to agree to as low a salary for as much work as possible. And yes, it takes confidence to seek a higher salary, but if you do not ask for more money, you will not get it!

Seven Big Mistakes People Make During Job Negotiations

"I've been rich and I've been poor; rich is better."
—Sophie Tucker, vaudeville entertainer, 1884–1966

A friend told me about a frustrating negotiation she had with her employer. After two initial discussions about job responsibilities and salary, the interviewer said he was close to offering her the position but needed to clear his decision with his boss. However, two weeks later, she still hadn't heard from anyone at the company. In addition, she still hadn't discussed her compensation package.

By the time the man made an offer—another week later—my friend wanted the job so badly that she not only accepted a number from the lower end of her salary range but also agreed to the company's "boilerplate" compensation package.

MISTAKE #1: Leaving discussion of the compensation package or other demands until after the job offer

If you only discuss salary before you accept a job offer and talk about other forms of compensation afterward, you have lost much of your negotiating power. This is a bit like closing the barn door after the horse has run away—it's too late to do anything about it.

Correction: Never accept a salary offer before you discuss all aspects of the job. Ask for everything you want early on in the negotiations so the employer can include as many of them as possible in his or her initial job offer.

> Say, "Let's put the salary on the backburner for the time being. I also want to talk about the full benefits package, the job responsibilities, a flexible work schedule, plus several other issues."

MISTAKE #2: Locking into a fixed negotiating position, such as salary or the job description

Negotiating a job from one fixed position leaves you without options if the employer does not make you an offer or refuses to give you what you want.

Correction: Tell your interviewer that you want to discuss alternatives and other forms of compensation.

Say, "I'm not locked into a fixed position here. Let's see what other alternatives and options we can come up with that we can agree on."

MISTAKE #3: Not anticipating an employer's objections to your salary or compensation requests

When you apply for a job, you are really selling yourself and your skills to a prospective employer. One important sales secret is having an answer ready for any possible objection a potential buyer might have. You can apply this sales strategy as you discuss your salary or compensation package.

Correction: Anticipate sticky issues that might prevent an employer from agreeing to your demands so you are prepared to suggest alternatives.

Say, "I thought that might be a problem, so I came up with this other option."

MISTAKE #4: Being overly aggressive or arrogant in the negotiation

Thinking big and asking for what you want in a job negotiation show confidence. However, making extreme demands or saying that you are considering several other job offers can easily backfire. Remember, the interviewer is thinking, *"Is this person someone I (or my fellow employees) will want to work with?"*

Correction: Adopt a friendly but businesslike approach to your job negotiations. Be assertive—not aggressive—when you say what you want. Your goal is to show the interviewer that you want to find the right combination of alternatives and options to reach a win-win agreement.

Say, "Let's discuss what each of us wants and then work out a job description and compensation package that will satisfy both of us."

MISTAKE #5: Not clarifying the employer's needs

Without knowing some of the issues and problems that your potential employer is facing, it will be difficult for you to offer him or her any specific solutions.

Correction: Probe for the company's most pressing issues. Listen carefully for and identify the top areas you feel most qualified to do something about.

Ask, "I know the industry, but your company has its own special needs. What are the biggest challenges facing this company in the area where I would be working?"

MISTAKE #6: Being overeager to accept a job offer

Negotiating a great job offer is a little like the old saying, "Know when to hold 'em, know when to fold 'em." Accepting a job offer too early in the negotiations almost certainly means that you left money or benefits on the negotiating table.

Correction: Secretly you might want the job so badly that you'd take any offer the employer makes, but put on your best poker face until you negotiate the best salary and compensation package you can—then smile!

Say, "Let me give it some thought."

MISTAKE #7: Accepting a job offer that is worse than your walk-away option. (The biggest mistake of all!)

The old adage, "A bird in the hand is worth two in the bush," will not get you a great job offer. Many employers will make the lowest possible offer with the hope that you will sell your valuable skills and experience at rock-bottom prices. If you accept a job on those terms, don't expect any concessions or benefits later.

Correction: Choose your walk-away option with the knowledge that it is a better alternative than taking a poor offer.

Say, "If that is your best and final offer, then I'm going to say no."

How to Use Silence and Stalling to Negotiate Better Job Offers

The Irish playwright Oscar Wilde (1854–1900) was a master of understatement. He explained the power of silence this way: "He knew the precise psychological moment when to say nothing." The next time you negotiate, use these two "quiet" strategies.

THE SILENCE STRATEGY

Silence is golden—as every negotiator knows. You can use silence in a variety of situations to strengthen your position. For example, you can remain silent after:

- Rejecting the first job offer. Your silence can elicit an even better second offer. It says, "I'm waiting for you to sweeten the deal."

- Asking for a trade-off. Your silence says, "You won't get a concession from me without offering me something in return."

- Hearing an unreasonably low job offer. Your silence says, "You are going to have to do a lot better than that if you want me to work for this company."

THE STALLING STRATEGY

Stalling is another negotiation strategy that can inspire a better job offer. By waiting, you can sometimes inspire your prospective employer to increase your salary or sweeten your compensation package. You can say:

"There are some financial details in your offer that I'm still discussing with my accountant (attorney, financial advisor, etc.)."

"My spouse and I are still talking about how our life at home would change if I take this job."

Stalling can also suggest that you are waiting for an offer from another company. You can say:

"I'd like more time to decide. I'm still considering my options."

"Keep up appearances, there lies the test; the world will give thee credit for the rest."

—Charles Churchill, British poet, 1731–1764

Negotiation strategies that lead to great job offers begin with preparation. Knowing the critical questions to ask and answer will improve your bargaining position and salary offers. Avoid the most common mistakes people make during job negotiations, use silence and stalling as negotiating strategies and you'll get a good job offer.

CHAPTER NINE

Talking Your Way to Successful Selling

"A living is made by selling something that everyone needs at least once a year. A million is made by selling something that everybody needs every day."

—Thorton Wilder, American dramatist, 1897–1975

In this chapter, you will learn:
• ABCs of successful selling • Dos and don'ts to glide past gatekeepers • Seven steps to effective cold calling • Three-step strategy to overcome objections • Twelve characteristics of top sales professionals

Walter, the Seltzer Man, is the third-generation owner of a water delivery business in New York City. He delivers bubbly water in the traditional thick glass bottles to each customer's door, just like his father and grandfather did before him. Walter's oldest customer, Mrs. Glitz, has been buying seltzer since Walter's father had the route. She explained why she is still a loyal customer: "The seltzer is great, but the thing about his product is that he's the product. It's about Walter."

Walter's story proves that the old sales maxim is true, "You're always selling yourself, no matter what product you're actually selling." However, what if you are a newcomer in the sales field or a veteran who needs some brushing up? What are the basics?

ABCs of Successful Selling

"There is only one cure for gray hair. It was invented by a Frenchman. It's called the guillotine."

—P. G. Wodehouse, British humorist, 1881–1975

Showman P. T. Barnum (1810–1891) was known for using wild antics to attract crowds of spectators to his circus shows. However, you do not need to be a fast-talking showman to be a successful salesperson. Skillful selling is based on this simple *A-B-C* formula:

A = ASK QUESTIONS ABOUT CUSTOMER'S WANTS AND NEEDS

One common mistake new salespeople make is that they attempt to sell their product or service *before* they listen to what their customer wants and needs. Avoid this pitfall by asking questions like:

"What is your biggest staff (supply, etc.) problem?"

"What do you see as the main challenges your department faces in the next few months (year, five years, etc.)?"

"What is it about the . . . you are using now that you're not happy with?"

B = "BENEFITS" BEFORE "FEATURES"

Once you know your customer's wants and needs you must convince him or her that you have the right solution. This is where many new salespeople make another classic selling mistake. They try to oversell the "features" (bells and whistles) instead of highlighting the "benefits" of their product or service. Sales pros know that customers are more likely to buy if they believe that the benefits of a product or service will help them fulfill their wants or needs.

The following examples show how to highlight product benefits before describing its features:

"Because you said you wanted a safe and economical space heater for your home (wants and needs), let me show you one of our most popular units."

"This super-efficient (benefit) heater has superior heating power (benefit). It can keep even the largest room in your house warm and cozy while saving you money on the bill (benefit). And—most important—it has no exposed heating elements (feature), so you have peace of mind (benefit)!"

"This heavy-duty oil-filled radiator heater (feature) has an automatic timer (feature), adjustable thermostat (feature), three variable settings (feature) and large, sturdy wheels (feature) so you can easily move it anywhere in your home (benefit)."

Using this technique you first uncover your customer's needs, then present the benefits. Next, describe your product's or service's special features and answer any questions. But to make the sale, you need to do more.

C = CLOSE THE DEAL BY ASKING FOR THE SALE

Many salespeople fail to take the most important step in the sales process—asking for the sale. Perhaps they fear rejection, do not want to appear too pushy or are just embarrassed. However, if a salesperson does not ask for a sale, the customer probably will not offer to buy. And that means "No sale!" To make that sale, take the risk and ask:

"How many do you want?"

"Shall I wrap it up, or do you want to wear it?"

"Would you like to pay for this in cash or put it on your credit card?"

"When can we start?"

"Where do you want me to send the order?"

You might get a "no" answer (See "Three-Step Strategy to Overcome Objections," later in this chapter), but your customer might just surprise you and say "Yes"!

Now that you know the ABCs of successful selling, you're ready to learn how to get past every salesperson's nightmare—the gatekeeper!

Dos and Don'ts to Glide Past Gatekeepers

"Nothing is as irritating as the fellow who chats pleasantly while he's overcharging you."

—*Kin Hubbard, American humorist, 1868–1930*

How many times have you tried to talk to a prospective client, only to be sent away by that person's assistant? Getting past the gatekeeper is always a challenge. Gatekeepers are secretaries, assistants, receptionists, security guards and other office personnel who faithfully screen their bosses' callers and visitors to keep out riffraff, pests or cold callers like you. Successful salespeople know the right words to say to get past vigilant gatekeepers. Here are several dos and don'ts to get past gatekeepers to decision-makers.

DO BE POLITE AND USE THE GATEKEEPER'S NAME

Gatekeepers often identify themselves when they answer the telephone, but if not, ask for his or her name. Make a note of the name and repeat it during your conversation. Remember it for next time, because you might need to call several times before the gatekeeper lets you through to a decision-maker.

Always be friendly, respectful and thank him or her for their help. A little humility goes a long way with gatekeepers. You can always ask him or her for assistance by saying, "Darlene, I've got a problem and I sure could use your help," or "Charles, what is the best way to contact your boss?"

DO HAVE A GOOD REASON FOR YOUR CALL

A good reason for calling can also get you past the gatekeeper. If you use one of the following responses to the gatekeeper's question, "What is this call in reference to?" your chances of talking to your prospect improve.

- Referred by a colleague:

    "Hello, this is . . . Helen Smith at . . . asked me to call Mr. Mansfield today. May I speak with him?"

- The prospective client requested a call:

    "Ms. Jones asked me to give her a call the first thing Monday morning. Is she in her office?"

- Returning a call:

    "I am returning Ms. Francisco's call. I know she hates playing telephone tag as much as I do. Is she free at the moment?"

DON'T:

- Fib and say you are a friend of the boss.
- Falsely claim you have an appointment.
- Fabricate a contact or prior conversation.

DO SPEAK WITH A SENSE OF URGENCY OR SERIOUSNESS

Because the gatekeeper's job is to let through important calls, if you sound serious or a bit urgent, your chances of being passed along to the decision-maker might improve. Say:

"Good morning, this is. . . . I need to talk to your boss right away—just for a minute. Is she in?"

"Good afternoon, this is. . . . I've been trying to get in touch with Ms. Bee for the last several days. It's important that I talk to her. Is she available?"

DON'T:

- Be dramatic or say there is an emergency.

- Bully, threaten or intimidate gatekeepers.

- Be unfriendly, aggressive or disrespectful to gatekeepers.

OTHER WAYS AROUND GATEKEEPERS

Do call at off-hours

Telephone or visit an hour before or after normal office hours or during the gatekeeper's lunch hour. This strategy works because many executives and purchasing managers work earlier or later than their gatekeepers do and often eat lunch at their desks. You can say:

"Hello Ms. Dee, I'm glad I caught you before your office opens (after hours, etc.). My name is. . . . I'm with EZ Corp. May I take a minute of your time?"

Don't waste your prospective client's time with small talk, exaggerated claims or long explanations

Do send an e-mail

An e-mail requesting a personal appointment or a good time to call can help you get you past the gatekeeper. If the gatekeeper refuses to give you the person's e-mail address, ask for the company website. Chances are, you will see other e-mail addresses on the site. Use the same format (i.e., first initial, last name @ companyname.com) with the person's name you want to contact. You can write:

Dear Mr. Thomas:

My name is . . . and I am with VORTEX TECHNOLOGY. We specialize in e-business integration solutions. I am going to be in your neighborhood next week, and I'd like to call or visit you Tuesday or Wednesday afternoon.

I'll only take a few minutes of your time to show you how our web applications server can solve your company's most complicated inventory, fulfillment and upgrading problems. Please send me a reply and let me know which day and time is best for you: Tuesday at 2 P.M. or Wednesday at 3 P.M.?

I'm looking forward to helping you make your company a superbly efficient integrated e-business.

Thank you,

(Your name and contact information)

Don't:

- Click "Send" without first checking your e-mail for grammar and spelling errors.

- Spam your prospects with promotions or newsletters.

- Hound prospects with e-mail requests for meetings.

Do send a small gift or novelty item

It is a gatekeeper's job to throw away much of the ordinary direct mail sent to his or her boss. However, if you send your prospective client something that might capture his or her attention, your chances of getting past the gatekeeper increase. For example, to reach the decision-makers, an author friend sent autographed copies of his book about customer service as gifts to the CEOs of the Fortune 100 companies. As a result, he got his foot in the door to the sales department and eventually made bulk sales of his book to several of the companies.

If you do send your prospective clients gifts or novelty items, be sure they:

- Are appropriate and tasteful.

- Communicate something about your product or service.

- Arouse the curiosity (not ire) of your client.

Don't:

- Go to extremes to get a response.

- Send items that might offend or send the wrong message to your prospects.

- Send expensive gimmicks or gifts without first determining how many sales you will need to make to recoup your costs.

Getting past gatekeepers presents a constant challenge to sales professionals. But once you get through to your prospect, you have the opportunity to make the sale—if you are ready with the right words!

Seven Steps to Effective Cold Calling

"Well if I called the wrong number, why did you answer the phone?"
—James Thurber, American cartoonist, 1894–1961

In the 1987 movie *Wall Street*, the young broker Bud Fox (played by Charlie Sheen) works the telephones to sell stocks to new clients. He makes hundreds of cold sales calls every day, yet he describes himself as an account executive. His father, Carl Fox (played by Martin Sheen), corrects him: "You get on the phone and you ask strangers for money—right? . . . You're a salesman!"

No matter what you sell, cold calling is a legitimate and effective way to reach potential customers and increase your sales. Many successful sales professionals make cold calling part of a prospecting strategy because they know it works. Cold calling can work for you, too, if you use the following steps.

STEP 1: Say your prospect's name

Which should you use, your prospect's first or last name? Most business etiquette experts advise salespeople that if you don't know someone, use "Mr./Ms. . . . ," unless the prospective client suggests otherwise. This is particularly important if you speak to prospects from countries other than the United States.

STEP 2: Introduce yourself

STEP 3: Make a rapport-building statement

You can say, "I know that in your business it's tough to . . . (find reliable vendors, enforce safety regulations, train new help, etc.)."

STEP 4: Ask for one minute of your prospect's time

You can say, "I promise I'll only take one minute of your time to tell you about a software program that will decrease your business taxes. After one minute, if you don't want to hear another word, just say so and I'll say good-bye. May I continue?"

STEP 5: In less than 60 seconds, describe your product or service along with its benefits

You can say, "The reason I'm calling you this morning is to tell you about an innovative government program especially designed to help businesses like yours take advantage of state incentives and tax credits. Would you like to hear a few examples of other organizations like yours that have signed up for our service and saved lots of money?"

STEP 6: Ask a "yes or no" question as a trial closing

A "trial closing" is a short-answer test question that tells you whether your prospect is leaning toward saying yes or no to your offer. A "yes" answer to a trial closing moves the person closer to making a buying decision. The next step is to "close" the sale by asking him or her for the order or appointment. A "no" answer means that your prospect has "objections" that you need to answer before he or she will say yes. To use a trial closing during a cold call you can ask something like:

"Do you think the service (or product) I've described would help you?"

"About how many people in your office could benefit if you decide to go with this new software program?"

"Would you like to hear about the special offer we are making to companies like yours?"

STEP 7: Ask for the sale or appointment

Ironically, some salespeople get cold feet during a cold call when they reach this critical step—closing the sale. You might need to answer a daunting array of objections, but when you get a positive response to a trial closing, don't hesitate. Ask for the sale or an appointment. Say:

> "That's great! I knew you'd love this product. How many can I sign you up for?"

> "I'm happy you like the design and plans. When do you want to begin construction?"

If you take a prospective buyer's first "no" as a final answer, you are losing sales. However, if you know how to overcome their objections, you can turn a "no" into a "yes."

Three-Step Strategy to Overcome Objections

> *"If at first you don't succeed, try, try again—then quit. No use being a damn fool about it."*
>> —*attributed to W. C. Fields, American comedian and actor, 1880–1946*

Wouldn't it be great if your prospective buyer always said "yes" when you asked for an appointment or sale? Of course, that's not going to happen because many prospects make excuses or say "no" out of habit after hearing sales pitches. They are stalling, avoiding a decision or just hoping you will go away. Here is a three-step process for overcoming a buyer's objections:

Step 1: Paraphrase the objection and add the word *but*.

Step 2: Answer the objection.

Step 3: Ask again for the sale or appointment.

Restating the objection shows you are listening. Adding the word *but* says that you are not going away and that you are about to answer the objection. Asking again for the sale or appointment says that you are the kind of person who does not like to take "no" for an answer.

Here are examples of common objections and the steps you can take to overcome them:

Customer objection: "My budget was cut."

You: "I'm sorry to hear that your budget was cut, but (Step 1) . . . I can work with you on the numbers to save you money (Step 2). Can we meet on Monday after lunch, say around 2 o'clock?" (Step 3)

Customer objection: "I already have a vendor, but thanks anyway."

You: "I'm sure your present vendor is terrific, and it's great to be so loyal, but (Step 1) . . . I have an exclusive line of merchandise that you can't get from anyone else (Step 2). Can I send you a dozen and you can see how they sell?" (Step 3)

Customer objection: "I don't want to waste your time."

You: "Thanks, I don't want to waste my time either, but (Step 1) . . . in thirty minutes I can show you how our inventory control program works (Step 2). I'd like to come by your office Wednesday morning around 8 o'clock. I'll bring donuts and coffee and show you how the software works right on your computer. I promise I'll be out of your office by 9 o'clock." (Step 3)

Customer objection: "I'm swamped! I really don't have a minute to spare."

You: "I understand your time is precious, but (Step 1) . . . let me take you to lunch on Tuesday and in the time it takes to grab a bite to eat (Step 2), . . . I'll show you how our newest machine can cut your production time by more than 30 percent. What do you say?" (Step 3)

Here are some things you can say when a prospect hesitates to say "yes":

"Can you tell me what part of the program (solution, program, package, price, etc.) I've described that doesn't work for you?"

"What part of my proposal are you saying 'no' to?"

"Why would you turn down an opportunity to save money on your packaging costs?"

Making a cold call, getting an appointment, pitching your service or product and asking for the sale are the steps to making sales.

Now, are you ready to join the ranks of the top sales professionals?

Twelve Characteristics of Top Sales Professionals

During a radio interview on BBC, British hair stylist Vidal Sassoon (1928–) quoted one of his teachers: "The only place that success comes before work is in the dictionary." In addition to knowing that success does not come easily, top sales people do these things:

1. Ask probing questions before making their sale pitches.

2. Listen 80 percent of the time and speak only 20 percent of the time.

3. Focus on solutions, not sales.

4. Emphasize the benefits of their products and services.

5. Keep their sales message brief.

6. Speak at industry meetings about their expertise.

7. Actively hunt for prospects in business and social situations.

8. Tell colleagues their sales goals and their plans to achieve them.

9. Adjust their message when they fail to make a sale.

10. Position themselves as a resource.

11. Act as an ongoing information source that will improve buyers' profits, productivity and competitiveness.

12. Educate buyers about industry changes in regulations.

DO YOU HAVE WHAT IT TAKES TO BE A "BEST SELLER"?

There are many theories about the skills, traits and attitudes of successful salespeople. Warren Greshes is a master salesman and consummate professional speaker who swears by cold-call prospecting and says, "Don't count the yeses; count the nos." Ron Karr, another extraordinary salesman, professional speaker and author of *The Titan Principle: The Number One Secret to Sales Success,* says, "The secret is asking enough of the right questions." Barbara Corcoran, founder of New York's largest residential real estate company The Corcoran Group says about her super successful salespeople, "My highest-grossing agents know how to fail well. They fall hard, but they get up fast."

"Nothing succeeds like success."

—*Proverb*

To talk your way to a successful career in sales, you need to talk less and listen more. Ask questions about customers' needs, demonstrate the benefits of what you are selling and close the deal. Getting past the gatekeeper and cold calling present challenges, but that's why persistence and knowing what to and what not to say can really make a big difference in your paycheck.

CHAPTER TEN

Networking to Build
Business Contacts

"If you wish to appear agreeable in society you must consent to be taught many things which you already know."
                                        —Johann Kaspar Lavater, Swiss poet, 1741–1801

In this chapter, you will learn:
• **Networking in four easy steps** • **Networking etiquette in business and social situations** • **Seven ways to follow up on networking leads** • **Seven advanced networking strategies for high-level hobnobbing**

Networking! It's the marketing buzzword that everyone swears by. And it's a business tool that really works! No matter where you are—at a business seminar, an association meeting, health club or cocktail party—the right kind of networking can help you increase your business contacts and move your career and sales to the next level.

Whether you are a manager, salesperson, vice president or recent college graduate, your networking skills are one of your most valuable marketing tools. Now it's time to break the ice and start networking.

Networking in Four Easy Steps

"I remember your name perfectly, but I can't think of your face."
                                                              —Anonymous

A hotshot young businessman prided himself on remembering names but was embarrassed when he had failed to recall an associate named Mr. Souter while networking at a Rotary Club meeting.

"You can remember my name," Souter said, "if you think of me as the big man wearing the big suit. Just look for the biggest thing you see when we meet again and that will help you remember my name." At the next meeting the young man greeted his portly colleague, "Good evening, Mr. Butler."

Dale Carnegie was right when he said, "a person's name is the sweetest sound in any language." Just be sure you say his or her name right!

STEP 1: Introduce yourself and learn the person's name

When you first introduce yourself, do not worry about what you are going to say next. Instead, in the first five seconds, focus on the person's name, say it aloud and repeat it silently to yourself. Now think of the first person who comes to mind—a friend, relative, neighbor or celebrity—with the same name. (This is my favorite method for remembering names. I know this sounds odd, but it works!) Giving your full attention to the person you meet will inspire you to remember his or her name and will also help you build instant rapport.

You want to:

- Make contact.

- Show interest in the other person.

- Use and remember the name.

- Create rapport.

STEP 2: Seek information

What topic do business people like to talk about the most? Not surprisingly, the answer is usually themselves. Always give the people you meet a minute or two to reveal their interests before you talk about your products or services.

You want to:

• Get others to reveal their wants and needs.

• Let others shine and feel good about themselves.

• Make others believe that you are listening and interested.

• Identify potential business contacts.

Ask a few closed-ended and open-ended questions. Use them to direct the conversation to topics that relate to your expertise. Use an event you are attending or your surroundings as a springboard for conversation. For example:

"Are you a member of this organization?" (closed-ended)

"What part of the industry are you in?" (closed-ended)

"What kind of business are you in?" (closed-ended)

"What do you find the most interesting part of this event?" (open-ended)

"Do you have a specialty?" (closed-ended)

"Where do you see your industry (profession, clients, etc.) heading in the next few years?" (open-ended)

STEP 3: Make your "elevator speech"

Once you know something about the person you are speaking with, it's time for your "elevator speech." An elevator speech is a brief and memorable "soundbite" about your work and how it might benefit others. For example, after chatting for a minute, or if someone asks me what I do, I often say, "I'm a small talk expert. I help people and businesses increase their profits and productivity through better interpersonal communication skills."

It all takes place in about the time it takes to ride a few floors on an elevator. You can give your elevator speech anywhere you network or talk to people—even in an elevator!

Your goal is to pique the interest of the person you are talking to. Follow this up with a *brief* description of how you achieve these benefits. You want to:

- Reveal how you can help them.

- Briefly explain what you do and how you do it.

- Build their curiosity and interest in you.

STEP 4: Conclude your conversation with offers and requests

Before your end your conversation so you can continue to mix and mingle, ask to exchange business cards with the other person and offer to:

- Send follow-up materials. Say:

    "May I send you a copy of our special report?"

- Introduce him or her to a colleague. Say:

    "I know someone who might be interested in doing some business with you."

- Help him or her overcome a problem. Say:

    "Call me and I'll walk you through the setup for the accounting program."

Smart businesspeople know that networking is a two-way street. Therefore, it's perfectly acceptable to request:

- A time to discuss possible business opportunities. Say, "It seems like we may have some mutually beneficial business opportunities. May I give you a call early next week to talk about them?"

- An appointment to meet. Say, "I'll bring a few samples by your office. How about Tuesday morning?"

- A referral (if you think the other person feels comfortable enough with you to say "yes"). Say, "Do you know of two or three people I could call who might be interested in what I do?"

- An introduction. Say, "I'd really like to meet. . . . Would you mind introducing me?"

Networking is easy when you follow these four steps. However, you do need to be aware that the rules of networking etiquette are different in business and social situations.

Networking Etiquette for Business and Social Situations

"If there is anyone here whom I have not insulted, I beg his pardon."
—Johannes Brahms, German composer, 1833–1897

Have you ever met a person like this while networking at a business or social event? You've been chatting for a minute or so. Then you notice that the person is no longer looking at you but is glancing over your shoulder and scanning the room. You turn around to see who he or she is looking at and the next thing you hear is, "Nice talking to you. I've got to say hello to a friend."

You have just been dumped by a "networking shark," a person who will do almost anything to make a contact. Although different rules of networking etiquette apply to business and social settings, bad manners are offensive no matter where you are. Here are some ways you can avoid a networking faux pas.

NETWORKING ETIQUETTE IN BUSINESS SITUATIONS

It's smart to network in business situations. Right away, you can focus on topics related to your respective areas of expertise, including how clients, organizations and businesses have benefited from your product or service. However, don't leave your good manners at home. Avoid these blunders in etiquette when networking in business situations.

- Don't gossip or reveal personal or confidential information about a colleague or business.

Violate this rule of etiquette just once and no one will trust you with confidential information. Be firm if someone pumps you for privy information.

Do say: "Sorry, that's confidential."

• Don't badmouth a competitor's product or service.

Follow the adage, "If you don't have anything nice to say, then don't say anything at all." Nasty remarks about your competition make you look petty and unprofessional.

Do say: "There are many businesses that offer consulting services, but our company (or service) is unique, because we. . . ." This sets you apart from your competition.

• Don't talk nonstop about yourself or your business.

People who brag nonstop about themselves and their business during networking opportunities not only bore their colleagues, but rarely make productive contacts.

Do say: "Now that you know a little about what I do, I'm interested in learning more about you and your business."

• Don't hard sell.

Although you may ask for a contact or an appointment, don't be too aggressive. Nothing turns off new contacts faster than heavy pressure to buy something, have a meeting or get a referral.

Do say: "Can I give you a call next week to chat for a few minutes?"

• Don't get pushy about meeting socially.

Many businesspeople enjoy socializing with their clients and contacts, but don't make your invitation sound obligatory.

Do say: "I've invited a few clients and associates to a casual dinner at my place next Saturday night. It'll be fun. We'll have good food and you'll get a chance to meet some interesting people, too. Give me a call by Wednesday if you'd like to come."

NETWORKING ETIQUETTE IN SOCIAL SITUATIONS

Social situations can provide great opportunities for networking—if you do it the right way. Start out by chatting about general interest topics before you start talking business. Avoid these etiquette goofs while networking in social situations.

- Don't offer your product or service without first building rapport.

    Most people attend social gatherings to meet people, make friends and have fun—not to be sold a life insurance policy or buttonholed about potential investments or some other product or service.

    Do: Chat informally about a variety of topics such as sports, movies, travel, restaurants, cooking, hobbies, music, books, mutual friends, popular culture or business media stories to build rapport and trust before you launch into your elevator speech. Modify the speech so it doesn't sound like you're "working the room."

- Don't pass out business cards to everyone.

    Anyone who acts like a barker at a carnival trying to snag customers risks offending everyone in the room and might be left standing alone with no one to talk to.

    Do: Offer your business card to people who show an interest in your product or service or want to know how to get in touch with you. You can say, "Because you asked, here's my card. Give me a call."

- Don't pressure people to talk business.

    Overzealous networking can alienate potential clients and eliminate any possibility of future business. You can test a person's willingness to discuss a business topic by gently bringing it up in the conversation. If he or she avoids the topic, then suggest a call in a few days.

    Do say: "Sarah mentioned that you're in the market for a new home. I'm in the business, and maybe I can help you. This might not be the time to discuss it, but if you'd like, I can give you a call next week."

- Don't ignore unlikely prospects.

    "Networking sharks" swim through crowds at parties and in other social gatherings trolling for clients. When they meet someone they deem an unlikely prospect for their product or service, they quickly ditch that person and move on to someone else.

    Do: Spend at least a few minutes engaging in friendly conversation with everyone you meet because you never know who that person knows or how you might be useful. You can say, "I enjoy chatting with people like you because I always find out something interesting."

- Don't be offended if people try to pick your brain or pump you for free information.

    It's common for people to ask for free advice when they meet an attorney, doctor, accountant, broker or other professional at a party. Take their interest in you as a compliment and a business opportunity.

    Do: Offer some free advice and then say: "Of course, for me to give you the best advice, I need to understand your situation more clearly. Call me at the office or give me your telephone number and I'll call you. Then we can talk."

Now that you know how to meet people, network and make new business contacts, don't make the classic mistake of failing to follow up on your new leads.

Seven Ways to Follow Up on Networking Leads

"Opportunity, n. a favorable occasion for grasping a disappointment."
—Ambroise Bierce, American writer, 1842–1914

Charles M. Schwab, past president of Bethlehem Steel, tells this story of a nearly missed opportunity. "I had put off a phone call for nine months," the millionaire said, "so I decided to list it as my number-one task on my next day's agenda. That call netted us a $2 million order."

Of course, not every networking contact will result in a large order, but generally, the sooner you follow up on a lead, the better. Some follow-ups require more time and expense than others, but depending on the contact, the returns can be worth it. Here are seven ways to follow up after a networking event.

1. WRITE A QUICK NOTE OR SEND AN E-MAIL

Send a brief note soon after the event. It shows you enjoyed meeting the person and would like to maintain contact. Keep it simple and friendly. You might write something like:

> "I enjoyed meeting you at the . . . last week. What a great event! I hope you enjoyed it as much as I did and that we see each other again. Stay in touch and give me a call if you or anyone you know ever needs any . . . (your product or service) and I'll do the same."

Note: Whether you send a more formal letter via "snail mail" or an informal e-mail, always begin with "I enjoyed meeting you at the . . . a few days ago and chatting about. . . ." Always check your spelling and make sure you have the person's name right!

2. SEND AN ARTICLE OR USEFUL RESOURCE

Another easy way to follow up with a new contact is to send him or her a relevant article, telephone number, website or any other useful business resource. Again, keep it simple and helpful. You might say something like.

> "Here is the article and (website address, telephone number, etc.) I promised to send you. I hope you find them helpful. Stay in touch and give me a call if you or anyone you know ever needs any . . . (your product or service) and I'll do the same."

3. SEND A THANK-YOU NOTE FOR A CONTACT'S ADVICE

Smart networking includes listening to the advice and suggestions of the people you meet. A brief thank-you note to those people who were helpful is a natural follow-up and shows your appreciation for the advice. Here is what you might write in a thank-you note or e-mail:

> "I took your advice to call . . . for . . . (computer training, office space, etc.). We have an appointment to meet next week to discuss how we might work together. I've given your name to three of my clients who are looking for a . . . (sales rep, etc.) If you have any (legal, accounting, etc.) . . . questions about your business, or if I can help you in any other way, give me a call. Let's stay in touch."

4. DO A FAVOR

Once you get to know contacts and feel comfortable with them, introduce them to associates, possible clients and vendors. Do what you can to help others achieve their goals.

5. SEND A REFERRAL

Of course, the best follow-up for a contact is a referral. Just imagine how grateful a networking contact would feel if you called and said:

> "I met someone who might be interested in your product (or service). I mentioned your name and what you do, and she said she would like to talk to you. Give her a call and let me know how it works out. Of course, if you or anyone you know ever needs any . . . (your product or service), I always appreciate referrals and I'll continue to do the same for you."

6. SEND A GIFT

Everyone loves to get a present in the mail. If you have a sample of your product or small gift that represents what you do, then send it. For example, I often send new contacts a copy of one of my books. Yes, a gift can cost a few dollars, but it will impress the people you meet and encourage them think of you if they or someone they know needs your product or service.

Always remember to add in a note: "Stay in touch and give me a call if you or anyone you know ever needs any . . . (your product or service) and I'll do the same."

7. KEEP CONTACTS ON YOUR MAILING LIST

Sometimes it takes years for a networking contact to pay off. For example, I know one fitness trainer who sent dozens of updates, postcards, articles and promo pieces to one contact she met at a health club. Five years later, the contact, who was a meeting planner, hired the fitness trainer for a speaking engagement. Now that's patience!

When it comes to following up with networking contacts, the big message is that persistence pays! Sometimes the referral or favor comes back to you from another source. You might not get any business directly from a contact, but you might develop a friendship instead. I know one person who even married a man she met while networking at a convention!

Seven Advanced Networking Strategies for High-Level Hobnobbing

"A dinner lubricates business."
—Lord Stowell (William Scott), British lawyer, 1745–1836

When you have an opportunity to mix and mingle with high-powered or influential guests at a dinner party, a fund-raising event or another high-profile social engagement, you might want to use some advanced networking strategies. Gathering information before a special event can really pay off when it's time to make conversation. You can use these advanced networking strategies when you have an opportunity to do some high-level hobnobbing.

1. Get a guest list, member list or directory of the group whose function you will attend. Go online and do a search regarding the organization, guests or members you want to meet.

2. Send the guest speaker a brief e-mail saying that you are looking forward to the event and hope that you get a chance to meet. You can include a question that you hope they can answer. (You can ask the host for speaker's e-mail address or search the online white pages.)

3. Search for guests' websites or the websites of their companies or organizations. Do a search for any recent articles that mention the company, person or industry. Print out the articles, read them and be ready to talk about the issues affecting members of the group.

4. Ask the host or a member of the group to introduce you to two or three people attending who might benefit from meeting you. For example, after chatting for a few minutes you might ask "Would you mind introducing me to some of your associates . . . ?"

5. Tell the people you meet that you are familiar with their work, achievements, industry and even their favorite charity. You can say something like:

   "I'd really love to hear about a . . . (current project) you're involved in."

   "How did you get started?"

6. Ask these new acquaintances for their advice. Actively listen and let them "play the expert." Many successful businesspeople enjoy helping others achieve their goals. You can ask:

   "What advice would you give someone who is just starting in your business?"

7. Tell the person that you would like to send him or her "a little something" that you think he or she will find helpful, useful or interesting. Then ask for his or her card or address. This is also the right time to offer your card.

"It's not what you know, it's who you know."

—*Proverb*

Networking is an enjoyable and effective way to find new clients, build professional relationships and make mutually beneficial connections. If you are willing to meet some new people, engage in some friendly conversation and follow up on your contacts, you can become a successful networker, too.

PART II

Words That Win in
Consumer Situations

CHAPTER ELEVEN

The Fine Art of Complaining for Better Service

"The buyer needs a hundred eyes, the seller but one."

—*Proverb*

In this chapter, you will learn:
• ABCs of complaining • How to get great service in restaurants • How to get better service when booking hotel rooms • Common consumer complaints and how to get action • How to ask for your money back • How to respond when all else fails

My mother taught me everything I know about complaining and consumer service. I was ten years old when she explained her simple return policy: "If it's no good, then take it back. Exchange it or get your money back."

When we moved into a new neighborhood a short time later, I got my chance to test her policy. My mother said, "Don, please take this cottage cheese back to the store and ask to talk to the manager. Tell him that you are Trude Gabor's son, that the cottage cheese is bad and that you want another one. And don't forget to say, 'please' and 'thank you.'"

It did not take many more trips to the store until the manager recognized me and just gave me whatever I wanted. Even the barber knew he had better cut my hair short enough or I would be back on my mother's orders for a closer trim.

These lessons about consumer rights have served me well over the years. Even to this day, whenever I buy or receive something that I am not happy with, I return it. I always say, "I'd like to speak to the manager, please." (I think: "I'm Trude Gabor's son.") Then I'd say, "I'd like to exchange (or get a refund for) this. . . ." In all these years, I have never been refused, and I always say thank you. Thanks Mom!

ABCs of Competent Complaining

"The squeaking wheel gets the grease."

—*Proverb*

If you are like many nice people, you never complain about shoddy service from retailers, restaurants, hotels and other businesses. It's not that you don't want good service, it's just that you do not want to cause a scene, sound petty, get into an argument or cause the offending employee to be fired. Ironically, your concern and consideration—or lack of assertiveness—perpetuates the poor service consumers have grown to expect.

A = ASSERT YOUR RIGHTS TO GOOD SERVICE

If you are uncomfortable complaining about bad service, remember this. As a paying customer, you have the right to speak up and complain when:

- Products do not function properly, are damaged or not delivered when promised

- Waiters or waitresses are rude, unavailable or careless

- Meals are not hot or do not meet your reasonable expectations

- Hotels or restaurants do not honor their reservations, advertisements or promises

- Stores do not have the products they advertise

Does Being Assertive Make You Nervous?

Do you get butterflies in your stomach or do your palms sweat when you need to be assertive? Are you afraid that people will think you are too aggressive or that you will get into a confrontation if you speak up when you do not get the service you deserve?

If this describes you, keep these points in mind:

- You do not need to accept lousy service, but you do need to speak up and assert yourself.
- You have a right to complain about poor service.
- If you ask for what you want, you are more likely to get it.
- Assertive complaining does not mean you are aggressive—it only means that you are willing to speak up on your own behalf.

B = BE CALM, FRIENDLY AND POLITE, BUT FIRM

As frustrating as lousy service is, yelling at a surly waiter, careless worker or inattentive customer service representative rarely gets positive results. In many cases, the proverb, "Honey catches more flies than vinegar" applies when you complain. Here are a few tips to keep your cool when you complain about things that have gone wrong:

- Always ask for, repeat and write down the name of the person with whom you are speaking.
- Keep your voice in a neutral tone.
- Never use foul, abusive language or call the person a nasty name.
- Keep a smile on your face and use words such as, "Please," "Thank you" and "I appreciate your help."
- Be patient and see how the person handles your complaint before threatening further action.

Note: If the person you are complaining to ignores you or is rude, say, "I'd like to speak to your supervisor. What is his or her name?"

C = CLARIFY THE PROBLEM AND SAY WHAT WOULD SATISFY YOU

Complainers who get the best results do not make vague accusations or snide remarks about poor service. Instead, their complaints are specific so that a manager or customer service representative can correct the situation. Here is how to clarify the problem.

- Describe your complaint or problem in one or two sentences. The shorter, the better. For example:

  "In a nutshell, I am unhappy with the flowers I ordered from you last week."

- Offer relevant dates, dollar amounts, details, names and verbal exchanges without exaggerating or getting emotional. For example:

  "Last Monday I ordered a $35 bouquet for my mother-in-law's birthday. I specifically asked for long-lasting flowers, but most of the flowers in the arrangement lasted only two days."

- Omit irrelevant details or inflammatory comments.

- Describe what you expected before the problem arose. Remember to use the name of the person to whom you are speaking and those who have helped you previously.

Close your complaint on a positive note to show that you are willing to remain a customer—if the person can resolve your problem.

Knowing the ABCs of complaining can help you get better service when things go wrong. Most managers and customer service reps, when treated respectfully, will do their best to correct a problem. Remember that most mistakes are unintentional and that most businesses want to correct them as quickly as possible. But how do you get the service you want and deserve in the first place?

How to Get Great Service in Restaurants

"If this is coffee, please bring me some tea; if this is tea, please bring me some coffee."

—Abraham Lincoln, sixteenth U.S. president, 1809–1865

Several years ago, my wife and I had a disappointing dining experience, so I wrote a letter to the manager of this favorite restaurant in New York City. It began this way:

Dear Mr. . . .
   Perhaps it is because we have enjoyed so many wonderful meals at your restaurant over the past twelve years that we were so disappointed with our dining experience on the evening of Valentine's Day.

Without rancor or exaggeration, I explained that because my wife and I loved to dine there we felt especially let down that evening. The manager called me two days later with a sincere apology—no excuses. In addition, he extended an invitation to return to the restaurant as his guest. He said, "We want you back. Order anything on the menu. The meal's on us!"

Slow service, incorrect orders and disappointing meals rate high on diners' list of complaints. However, smart restaurant managers and owners say that when something goes wrong, they want to make it right. But that means you need to speak up.

When I asked Mike Albert, the manager of *John's Restaurant*, my favorite Italian restaurant in New York City, how he handles complaints, he said, "Most problems are easy to solve, but not if the manager doesn't know about them." He suggests that dissatisfied diners do the following:

- As soon as you realize you have a problem—receive the wrong order or improperly prepared meal, an undesirable table or an inattentive server—use eye contact or signal with your hand—not your index finger—to get the server or manager to come to the table. If you have trouble getting someone's attention, get up from the table and find the manager.

- Smile and say in a calm and polite voice:

  "We have a problem with one of our orders (our table, our server, etc.). Can you help us, please?"

- When the server asks, "What seems to be the problem?" explain the reason for your complaint without getting nasty or aggressive. You can say:

  "Usually when I order . . . it comes out just perfect, but not this time. Would you please bring us another one, and this time please ask the chef to make sure it is. . . . I appreciate it. Thank you."

  "I'm afraid there has been a mistake. I ordered . . . not. . . . Please take this away. Thank you."

  "This table is too close to the kitchen for us to enjoy our meal. Will you please find us another in a quieter part of the restaurant? Thanks, we'd really appreciate it."

  "I'm sorry to bring this to your attention, but I'm sure as the manager you want to know when someone on your staff is rude to one of your customers."

- Be prepared to wait a few extra minutes, but not too long. Say:

  "We'd really appreciate it if you can find us a better table in the next few minutes."

Once you speak up, be patient for your replacement meal or relocation to a new table. The staff might need a few extra minutes to solve the problem. If you are waiting longer than seems reasonable, motion to the waiter with wide eyes and a smile. Chances are, you will get just what you want.

How to Get Better Service When Booking Hotel Rooms

"Twenty-four-hour room service generally refers to the length of time that it takes for the club sandwich to arrive. This in indeed disheartening, particularly when you've ordered scrambled eggs."

—Fran Lebowitz, American humorist, 1950–

Comedian Bob Hope knew what it was like to stay in all sizes and sorts of hotel rooms. During one performance in a theater, he cracked this old joke about his current accommodations: "My room is so small, even the rats are round-shouldered."

The hotel proprietor was in the audience and became so upset by Hope's slam that he threatened to sue if the comedian did not retract his statement. The next evening, Hope opened his show with this apology. "I'm sorry I said the rats in my hotel are round-shouldered. They're not."

Anyone who has traveled knows how frustrating some hotels can be—especially after a long day on the road. Perhaps your hotel reservation has been cancelled so you are "walked" to another hotel. Or your "suite" turns out to be the size of a broom closet. Even worse, when you order room service, it takes hours to arrive. Then there is the greatest indignation of all—you discover that you paid far more for your room than you had to.

Of course, most hotels do their best, but there are several ways to ensure better service and lower rates. Here's what you can do to get a better rate on a hotel room:

- Call the hotel directly several times over the period of a few weeks. Depending on the time of year and the events in that location, prices differ from room to room and day to day. Ask:

    "What is your room rate today for . . . ?"

- Ask about promotions and special deals, especially group discounts for AAA (American Automobile Association), AARP (American Association of Retired Persons), convention attendees or others eligible for group discounts. Say:

    "Please tell me about any promotions or group specials you are offering now."

    Also ask, "Is that the best you can do?" Often the hotel sales representatives will throw in a few perks or premiums like a free breakfast or passes to local events, but only if you ask for them.

- Ask, "What exactly does the room have?" or "Can you describe the room to me?"

- Finally, once you agree to book the room, get a letter of confirmation. If the hotel is overbooked, it probably will not help you get a room, but it might get you a better room at a nearby hotel.

- Call three days before your booked date to confirm your reservation and any rate changes. If the rate has changed, cancel your original reservation and rebook or ask for credit for the difference in price. (Note: Be sure to check the cancellation policy, usually 24 to 72 hours.)

- If possible, deal with the hotel manager. Confirmed guests can be bumped, but those who have a relationship with the manager are usually not the first to go.

WHAT TO SAY IF YOUR HOTEL SAYS, "SORRY, WE'RE OVERBOOKED"

Savvy travelers know they cannot count on room reservations because hotels typically overbook in anticipation of guests who do not show up or cancel at the last minute. However, if all the guests do arrive, then the hotel will do what is called "walking the guest"—sending him or her to another hotel with a comparable room. If that happens to you, here's what you can say:

"I'd like to telephone home at no charge to notify my family of my new location."

"I expect the hotel to pay for the transportation to the new hotel."

"I expect the hotel to pay any extra cost of the new room."

"I certainly would appreciate a room upgrade, a nice gift basket or some extra points on my rewards program. How about it?"

Even when you know how to get a great hotel room at a great rate, there are other common situations where consumers get short shrift.

Common Consumer Complaints and How to Get Action

"The marvels of modern technology include the development of a soda can which when discarded, will last forever—and a $7,000 car, which when properly cared for, will rust out in two or three years."

—Paul Harwitz, cowboy poet

One of the goals of computers, voicemail, e-mail, tracking numbers and many other technological innovations in business was the promise to help consumers and improve customer service. Ironically, the opposite has proven true in many cases. It seems as if customer service has only deteriorated instead of getting better. But don't despair.

Here are three of the most common areas of customer complaints and what you can say or do to get some action. Remember to always ask for, write down and use the name of the person with whom you are speaking.

MAIL-ORDER COMPLAINTS

Complaints about mail orders abound—delayed orders, wrong items and damaged goods. If you have a problem with your mail order, give the company a call. Be sure you have all the ordering information ready for the customer service representative. Be polite and clearly state the problem, and, if necessary, be ready to cancel or request a refund.

Here is what you can say:

"Mr. Fry, I ordered two new pillows from your company on September 15 and was told they would be delivered within two weeks. Today is October 10 and the pillows have not been delivered. When can I expect them?"

"Ms. Lee, unfortunately, the computer you sent me was damaged, so I'd like to return it for another one. Can you help me with that? Here is my order number."

BILLING COMPLAINTS

If you don't keep a close eye on your bills, you might be charged an incorrect amount, double charged or even pay for someone else's purchase. That's why many businesses and credit card companies suggest that you look over the listed charges before you write a check or pay the bill. However, if you find an error on your statement or invoice, you can still do something about it.

Be sure to state all the pertinent facts, have copies of your statements, canceled checks, invoices and other relevant documents and say what action you want to solve the problem. Always be polite and respectful to the customer service representative and ask for his or her name.

Here is what you can say:

"I'm calling to question a charge on my bill. I'm sure it was a mistake, but the amount I was charged for the coffeemaker did not reflect the sale price according to the newspaper ad. I didn't notice the wrong price on my receipt until just now. I'd like to get a credit for the difference, please. Can you help me with that?"

"I hope you can help me with a billing mistake on my account."

FACILITY COMPLAINTS

If you belong to a gym, recreation center or health club facility, you do not deserve dirty showers, shabby changing rooms, broken equipment, unsafe conditions or discourteous staff. However, if that is what you encounter, do not suffer silently.

Here's what you can say:

"Diane, I have been a member of your fitness club for nearly four years, and for most of that time I have been happy with the facilities and service. However, recently, I have noticed a drastic decline in the club's overall service, particularly the maintenance of the equipment."

PRODUCT COMPLAINTS

Do you find that many products you use do not quite live up to your expectations or disappoint you in some way? Here is what I said when a pair of walking shoes I bought came with a little something extra that I didn't count on:

> "I'm calling you today because the pair of walking shoes I bought two months ago squeak loudly with every step. This problem started soon after I purchased the shoes. I thought the squeaking would eventually go away as I broke the shoe in, but it never did. Can you please help me?"

This shoe company knows a thing or two about great service. Of course, the customer service representative apologized for the problem—without putting the blame on me. Then she told me exactly how to send the shoes back to the factory—at the company's expense. A week later a new pair of walking shoes arrived in the mail. Thankfully, they were silent every step of the way!

BUILDING CONTRACTOR COMPLAINTS

Building contractors who specialize in home repairs and renovations often make promises they do not keep, particularly about the time it takes to complete a project. The best advice is to work only with licensed and insured contractors who have bona fide references and invite you to inspect work they have done for other clients. Be sure all the details of the job are in writing—including all specifications, costs, quality and markups on materials, start and completion dates, cleanup and all other details. Even when you cover all the bases, you might still have problems getting contractors to meet their obligations.

Threatening contractors can backfire, so first try cajoling them. You can say:

> "You came recommended as someone I could count on for professionalism, and we are happy with your work so far. However, when we paid you the advance and signed our agreement, you assured us

that you would complete the job by March 1. It's already February 15 and we are concerned that you won't finish in time for the wedding we have planned at the house on March 15. Will you finish on time as you agreed to in your contract?"

If a softer approach fails or your contractor has blatantly violated your contract (overcharged you for materials, failed to complete work on time or is guilty of poor workmanship, etc.), then you might need to threaten further action. Here is what you can say:

"Before we hired you to landscape our yard, we called your references and they gave you glowing praise. In our contract, you agreed to complete the work by April 1. However, now it is April 15, our entire yard is dug up and you and your workers have not been here for over a week."

"Because I have agreed to put my house up for sale on June 15, you have left me with little choice. If you or your men are not here working within two days (April 17), I will cancel our contract and get someone else to finish the job."

How to Ask for Your Money Back

"Advertising is the most fun you can have with your clothes on."
—Jerry Della Femina, advertising executive, 1936–

Have you received poor-quality products at outrageous prices? Have you waited too long for an undelivered item? Have you returned a product that never performed as advertised? Were you charged for something that you never ordered? When it comes to bad service, there's a limit, and you have reached it! Although the mistake might be unintentional, you have run out of patience—now is the time to ask for your money back, whether it is in person or over the telephone. Follow this direct three-step procedure:

SITUATION 1: Simple car repair that takes too long

Step 1: Briefly state the problem.

"Mr. Richfield, a week is much too long to wait for you to replace a tail light in my car."

Step 2: Offer a brief review of the facts.

"You promised me that if I paid you in advance, the job would be done by the next day. But for the last week my car's tail light has been sitting in your shop."

Step 3: Directly ask for your money back.

"Mr. Richfield, please just put the old light back, I'll pick up my car and the money I paid you and that will be the end of it."

SITUATION 2: The appliance that never worked right

Step 1: Briefly state the problem.

"Ms. Wheatley, the ad for Master Baker Breadmaker read, *Make homemade bread right in your own kitchen!* But unfortunately, this product was a real disappointment."

Step 2: Offer a brief review of the facts.

"When I turned on the bread maker it shook like an old jalopy. Then the baking element got so hot that the plastic parts on the outside of the unit got soft and began to melt. I don't think the bread maker is safe."

Step 3: Directly ask for your money back.

"Ms. Wheatley, I am returning the Master Baker Breadmaker machine in its original box and packaging. Your ad stated 'your satisfaction guaranteed,' and I'm definitely not satisfied. Please refund my purchase price of $175.86, plus $7.66 for shipping. I expect a check in the full amount of $183.52 to be promptly sent to me at my home address. Thank you."

SITUATION 3: The overdue refund

Step 1: Briefly state the problem.

"Ms. Penny, it has been seven weeks since I first brought the accounting error on my statement to the attention of your bookkeeping department. As of today, I still have not received the $65.98 credit to my account. Plus, to add insult to injury, today I received a delinquent payment notice in the mail."

Step 2: Offer a brief review of the facts.

"If you recall, Ms. Penny, I was charged for an item I did not purchase. When we spoke on Wednesday you promised me the matter would be taken care of. Now I am extremely upset to see that it was not."

Step 3: Say what you want them to do.

"Ms. Penny, I take great pride in paying my bills on time and having a spotless credit record. I'm sure you understand how important an accurate credit record is and I know that you will do everything in your power to correct your company's mistake as quickly as possible."

You now know how to ask for you money back, but what can you do if the business still ignores your complaints?

How to Respond When All Else Fails

"I am a kind of burr; I shall stick."
—William Shakespeare, British playwright, 1564–1616

A seemingly wise teacher invested her life savings in a business enterprise that—at the time—sounded like a great deal. "Your rate of return will be twice what you'd get for any other investment," the smooth-talking fellow had said, "and the beauty is, you can't lose!"

When the swindler and money suddenly disappeared, the teacher went to the Better Business Bureau, where her darkest fears about the man were confirmed.

"For goodness sakes," said the man from the bureau, "why didn't you come here before you invested all your money? Didn't you know about the Better Business Bureau?"

"Oh yes," she said, "but I was afraid you would tell me not to do it."

Have you asked for a product replacement or a refund that is ignored by the company or person you dealt with? Have you talked to a manager or even senior vice president who promises to handle the problem and then does nothing? Have you written letters explaining the problem, sent e-mails and faxed documents, and still have not received a refund, a product replacement or the service you ordered? Has the company you did business with disconnected its telephone or suddenly disappeared? If so, you need to take action to get satisfaction.

Note: When you demand satisfaction, *never* make personal threats or promise actions that you cannot or will not take.

A neatly typed letter addressed to the *president* of the company has a better chance of creating the desired impact than a telephone call. In your letter, include the following three parts:

Part 1: Recap the problem. (Attach relevant documents and previously written letters.)

Part 2: Say what you want, when you want it. Then explain what you are going to do if you do not get satisfaction.

Part 3: Tell the company to take action or face the consequences.

Here is what you can write.

Dear Mr./Ms. President:

(Part 1)

Because I have been unable to get any meaningful response from anyone in your company, I am writing to you as a last resort. After six weeks, your company has still not refunded my money (replaced the unit, fixed the billing mistake, repaired the damage, etc.). All relevant documents and my previous correspondence with your company regarding the problem are attached.

(Part 2)

I've run out of patience. If I do not get my money refunded (air conditioner replaced, billing mistake corrected, etc.) by (name the date), I'm going to take further action, including a formal letter of complaint about your company to all of the following:

• Your company's board of directors
• The Better Business Bureau
• Your industry associations
• The city attorney's office
• The state Attorney General's office
• Local media consumer advocates
• Local political representative
• My personal attorney

(Part 3)

Mr./Ms. President, I have sent you all the relevant supporting documents and you know exactly what I expect from you. You have the opportunity to put this matter to rest right now. I urge you to act now and save yourself more time and money, because I am not going away until you resolve this problem to my satisfaction.

I'm sure you understand what I want and would expect the same thing if you were in my position. I look forward to my refund (new computer, repaired ceiling, etc.) by. . . . I thank you with the hope that your company will do what is right and finally resolve this matter.

Sincerely,
Your name

When all else fails, writing a letter to the head of the company is probably the only way to get someone to act on your behalf. After all, don't most company presidents believe in Harry Truman's motto, "The buck stops here"?

"If it sounds too good to be true, it probably is."

—*Proverb*

Remember, knowing the people and businesses you deal with and their return or exchange policies makes it easier to deal with problems if they arise.

Whether you use the telephone, write letters or appear in person, you can get better customer service if you know the right ways to complain. It isn't always easy, but when you are specific, have a polite but firm voice and refuse to take "no" for an answer, you'll be surprised just how often you will get what you ask for—and deserve.

CHAPTER TWELVE

Talking to Doctors, Nurses and Other Health-Care Professionals

"My doctor told me that jogging would add years to my life. I think he was right. I feel ten years older already."

—Milton Berle, American comedian, 1908–2002

In this chapter, you will learn:
• **Five tips for a productive doctor's visit** • **Eight questions to ask your doctor before you agree to a major procedure** • **Dos and don'ts when talking to doctors** • **How to complain about a doctor, nurse or other health-care professional** • **How to thank your doctor, nurse or other health-care professional**

A doctor asked a new patient during his first visit, "And whom did you see about this problem before me?"

"My pharmacist," the man replied.

"And what useless advice did he give you?" the doctor asked, not hiding his superior attitude.

The man smiled, "He suggested that I come and see you."

Let's face it, some doctors can, at times, be intimidating. However, when you are ill, whom else are you going to call?

Five Tips for a Productive Doctor's Visit

"The best doctors in the world are Dr. Diet, Dr. Quiet and Dr. Merryman."

—Jonathan Swift, Irish author, 1667–1745

Visiting the doctor can be a nerve-wracking experience, but if you prepare for your appointment, you can cover all the important questions or points that are easy to forget if you are feeling anxious. Keep these five tips in mind:

1. Make a list of all your questions and needs, including new prescriptions, renewals, flu shot, etc.

2. Have a list of all the medications you take—prescription and over-the-counter—plus any nutritional supplements and vitamins.

3. Write down a list of your symptoms and the times, dates, diet, lifestyle, medical history, personal events and any other relevant information that might help your doctor make the best diagnosis and prognosis.

4. Ask a friend or family member to come along. Four ears are better than two, especially if you are discussing complicated procedures or serious illnesses.

5. Take careful notes about what your doctor says.

You will need to pay close attention once your doctor explains your condition and suggests possible remedies. Taking notes helps you remember important details and allows you to examine your options later with a friend or family member at home.

You now know some tips for visiting a doctor. Once you are in the office, your doctor might offer you a diagnosis of your problem and suggest a treatment. However, before you make any major decisions, you need to ask him or her several important questions.

Eight Questions to Ask Your Doctor Before You Agree to a Major Procedure

"After two days in the hospital, I took a turn for the nurse."
                                    —W. C. Fields, American actor, 1879–1946

During an exhaustive medical examination, Otto, Archduke of Austria (1865–1900), became irritated by the doctor's many questions about his symptoms, pains and personal habits. After the Archduke complained, the doctor replied, "Your Highness, I suggest that the next time you feel ill, you call for a veterinarian. He cures without asking any questions."

Of course, your doctor asks you questions to help determine an accurate diagnosis and a remedy for your medical problem. However, you need to ask several questions of your own to make an informed decision about treatment. Here are the eight most important questions to ask your doctor if you are considering a major medical procedure:

1. "WHAT IS YOUR OPINION OF MY CONDITION?"

Ask your doctor to clearly explain your condition. Do not be afraid to ask him or her for further clarification, to define confusing or unfamiliar terms or to explain something again if you do not understand.

You can say:

"I don't know what . . . means."

"I don't understand. What does . . . mean exactly?"

"Can you draw me a simple picture or diagram that shows me the problem and what the operation will accomplish?"

"I don't understand. Will you explain it to me again?"

"Do you have any literature I can read that will help me understand the procedure better?"

2. "WHAT OPTIONAL PROCEDURES, OPERATION OR COURSE OF TREATMENT DO YOU RECOMMEND?"

Once your doctor tells you his or her opinion, he or she will probably suggest one or more possible courses of action. It is important to ask:

"What other options are open to me?"

"What are the differences between the treatments?"

"Which course of action do you favor and why?"

3. "WHAT DO I HAVE TO GAIN BY HAVING THIS PROCEDURE?"

Knowing the benefits you can expect from a treatment helps you make the best decision. Ask:

"How will this procedure help me?"

"How long will the benefits last?"

"Realistically, how much can I expect my condition to improve?"

4. "WHAT IS INVOLVED IN THE OPERATION?"

You do not need to hear all the vivid details, but your doctor can give you the "big picture" of what he or she proposes to do. Ask:

"What kind of anesthesia will you use?"

"Where does the procedure take place?"

"About how long will the procedure take?"

"What is the recovery time?"

"What kind of pain or side effects can I expect?"

"Will I need any special help or home care afterward?"

"What is the follow-up after the procedure?"

"When and how many times will I see you afterward?"

5. "WHAT ARE THE RISKS?"

Nearly all medical procedures, treatments, drugs and operations have elements of risk. You need to know what these risks are before making the best decision. Ask:

"What kind of complications can occur?"

"Can the pain (infection, rash, etc.) get worse?"

"What has been your past experience with cases like mine?"

"Given my state of health, what are my chances of having a successful outcome?"

6. "WHAT IF I DON'T DO ANYTHING ABOUT MY CONDITION?"

In certain situations, taking a "wait and see" approach might be wise. Ask your doctor:

"What will happen if I do nothing?"

"How long do I have to make a decision?"

"Will this problem go away over time without surgery (treatment, drugs, etc.)?"

"Am I risking a greater problem if I elect to forgo surgery (treatment, drugs, etc.)?"

7. "HOW MUCH WILL THIS PROCEDURE COST?"

Be sure to check with your health insurance company to see if your policy covers the treatment, drugs, surgery, etc. your doctor recommends. You can ask:

"Do you take . . . insurance?"

"What do your fees cover?"

"How will I be billed?"

8. "HOW DO YOU FEEL ABOUT ME ASKING ANOTHER DOCTOR FOR A SECOND OPINION?"

Be sure to check with your insurance company before you seek a second opinion. You can say:

"Before I commit to this procedure, I'd like to get a second opinion."

"This is a lot of complicated information for me to digest. I need a second opinion before I'm ready to decide which treatment is best for me."

You now know how to prepare for you doctor visit. However, remember that how you talk to your physician can make a difference in the care you receive.

Dos and Don'ts When Talking to Your Doctor

"I would have killed myself but my analyst was a strict Freudian and if you kill yourself they make you pay for the sessions you miss."
—Woody Allen, American comedian, 1935–

Konrad Adenauer (1876–1967), first chancellor of the Federal Republic of Germany after World War II, had contracted a serious cold as he neared his ninetieth birthday. The impatient Adenauer chided his personal physician for not being able to relieve his symptoms.

"I'm not a magician," the doctor snapped, "I can't make you young again!"

"I haven't asked you to," Adenauer replied. "All I want is to go on getting older."

Sharp words or impatient behavior will only annoy your doctor and make him or her less attentive to your needs. That is why it is important to follow these dos and don'ts when you talk to your doctor.

Do:

- Describe your problem briefly and accurately. Doctors are not mind readers.

- Be honest about what is bothering you and how long you've had the symptoms, even if it may be embarrassing.

- Listen carefully and allow your doctor to finish speaking before you ask questions. Then ask for clarification, specifics or further explanation.

- Be aware of the doctor's time. Sure, you want to have his or her complete attention, but do not go into excruciating detail or go off on a tangent when discussing your medical problem.

- Check for your understanding by restating what you think the doctor has told you and what you should do.

Don't:

- Offer your own diagnosis—just describe your symptoms.

- Expect doctors to be miracle-workers or magicians. Keep your expectations realistic.

- Get angry or belligerent if the doctor tells you what you do not want to hear.

- Complain about other doctors to your doctor.

- Ignore your doctor's advice.

You now know some dos and don'ts and how to talk your doctor. However, what can you do if you are not satisfied or if you disagree with his or her opinion or treatment? It might be time to find another doctor to handle your problem.

How to Complain About a Doctor, Nurse or Other Health-Care Professional

"He has been a doctor a year now and has had two patients, no, three, I think—yes it was three: I attended their funerals."

—Mark Twain, American humorist, 1835–1910

Even the best doctors and health-care professionals sometimes slip up when it comes to good customer service. However, you do not need to take bad service lying down. You have the right to speak up if you are unhappy or dissatisfied with a doctor, nurse or other health-care professional. Here is what you can say:

I. STATE ALL THE RELEVANT FACTS

If a doctor, nurse or other health-care professional mistreats you or fails to provide you with proper care in any way, make a note of the date, time, people involved and the situation. Be specific, state only relevant facts and quote the offending person accurately. Stay calm and express your complaint to the head doctor or person in charge in a neutral tone of voice. Getting emotional will only undermine your case. Here are other words or phrases you can use to voice your complaint:

"I think you should know that. . . ."

"I want to call your attention to. . . ."

"I was unhappy when your assistant told me to. . . ."

"I was angry at the way I was treated."

2. MAKE ANY SUGGESTIONS YOU THINK WILL RECTIFY THE SITUATION

Most doctors, nurses or other health-care professionals will be open to your suggestions. However, because you might not know the true source of a particular problem, limit your comments to how you would have preferred to be treated, instead of specific remedies.

For example, an elderly patient could say:

"Doctor, the automated telephone system at your office is extremely frustrating, especially for patients like me who need to talk to a doctor or a real person. Perhaps you can set up your system so that your patients can talk to someone right away. Also, perhaps you would remind the person answering the telephone to be more sensitive to your patients' concerns when they call."

Here are other phrases you can use when offering a suggestion:

"If I may make a suggestion. . . ."

"Perhaps if you changed. . . ."

"One thing that might prevent the problem from occurring again would be to. . . ."

"Perhaps you could remedy the situation if you. . . ."

3. EXPRESS YOUR CONFIDENCE THAT THE PROBLEM WILL BE DEALT WITH

Doctors, nurses or other health-care professionals need to know that if you are to retain their services, you expect them to take appropriate steps to remedy the problem. This is not a threat, but simply points out that you have a choice of health-care providers. Here is what you can say:

"If this problem has happened to me, I'm sure it's happened to some of your other patients, too. I'm sure you want your patients (clients) to avoid this problem in the future."

Here are other phrases you can use to tell your doctor you expect some changes.

"I hope this problem doesn't happen again."

"Over the years, I have been happy with your care, so I hope that you'll see to it that this problem is solved."

"I really appreciate you giving this problem your prompt attention."

HOW TO THANK A DOCTOR, NURSE OR HEALTH-CARE PROFESSIONAL

"My doctor is wonderful. Once in 1955 when I couldn't afford an operation, he touched up the X rays."

—Joey Bishop, American comedian and actor, 1918–

After fainting several times, Frank Sinatra consulted with his doctor to find out the source of the problem. After a careful physical examination of his patient, the doctor asked, "How much money do you earn, Mr. Sinatra?"

Be Nice to Your Nurse

If you are in the hospital, you need and count on your nurses nearly every hour of the day and night. Starting your relationship off on the right foot will make your hospital stay more pleasant and help you get better faster. Here are some tips on how to get along better with nurses:

- Be friendly, cooperative and respectful.

- Work together as a team so you can get better faster.

- Your nurse may be able to make a procedure more comfortable if you say how you feel and offer a suggestion on how you prefer the procedure done.

- Although your nurse is not a doctor, she might be able to answer some of your medical questions.

- Patients in the hospital sometimes get angry. Do not take your anger out on the nurses who care for you.

- Remember that nurses must follow strict procedures or treatments that you might not like but that are designed to help you get better faster.

- Keep your sense of humor and chat with your nurse about her interests.

"Somewhere between a four hundred thousand and a million dollars a year," the crooner answered. "Why do you ask?"

"In that case," his doctor advised, "I suggest you go right out and buy yourself some red meat. You're suffering from malnutrition."

Of course, being a doctor, nurse or other health-care professional requires enormous skill and knowledge. However, even if his or her advice is nothing more than common sense, he or she deserves your gratitude. Unfortunately, most patients only complain. It's never too soon or too late to tell a doctor, nurse or other health-care professional when things go right. Like most people who strive to do a good job, they will welcome a compliment from you. Here is what you can say in three easy steps:

- Say right away that your comments are positive.

    "I want to tell you how happy I was with the treatment and service I received at your office during my recent visit."

- Here are other phrases you can use to express your appreciation:

    "I want you to know how much I appreciated. . . ."

    "Thank you so much for your efforts on my behalf."

    "Health-care professionals like you and your staff are rare, and I just want to thank you for. . . ."

- State clearly how you benefited from the actions of doctor, nurse or other health-care professional.

Be specific when you offer a compliment so he or she knows exactly why you feel so positive about your experience. For example:

    "I was so nervous when I walked into your office, but your nurse made me feel so welcome and comfortable that I almost forgot why I was there."

    "Before you helped me with my physical therapy, I felt like I was ready for the nursing home. But you made me realize that I am more independent than I thought."

- Seeing a therapist or other mental health-care professional can last for many months or even years. However, at some point you may decide to discontinue seeking his or her professional advice. Here is what you can say:

    "I want to thank you for everything you've done for me over the last several months (years). I feel that now I can get on with my life on my own."

    "I feel I've benefited from my sessions with you, but I've decided to make this my last session."

- Here are other complimentary phrases you can say to a doctor, nurse or other health-care professional:

    "You've really improved my ability to. . . ."

"I feel so much better since you. . . ."

"You have made a big difference in my life."

"I really appreciate everything you have done for me."

• Thank them again.

Once you have complimented your doctor, nurse or other health-care professional, as a final gesture of gratitude, simply say:

"I want you to know how thankful we are for your kindness and dedication. Thank you so much for everything that you have done for us."

"Thanks again for everything you've done for me."

"I am so grateful for all your efforts. Thank you."

"All your work has made a big difference in my life. I can't thank you enough."

"The unruly patient makes a harsh physician."
—*Publilius Syrus, Roman dramatist, first century* B.C.E.

A few words of appreciation go a long way with doctors, nurses and other health-care professionals. You will get the most benefit from your doctors, nurses or other health-care professionals with the least frustration and anxiety when you communicate clearly and listen carefully. When that happens, they are in the best position to help you live a long and healthy life.

CHAPTER THIRTEEN

Talking to Lawyers, Police
Officers and Traffic Judges

"It ain't no sin if you crack a few laws now and then, just as long as you don't break any."

—Mae West, American actor, 1892–1980

In this chapter, you will learn:
• **Questions to ask** *before* **you hire an attorney** • **Ten biggest mistakes clients make when working with an attorney** • **How to save money on legal fees** • **Five strategies that (maybe) will keep you from getting a traffic ticket** • **Twelve things you should** *never* **say to a police officer** • **Six ways to beat a traffic ticket**

In his book, *A Writer's Notebook,* Somerset Maugham (1874–1965) tells the story of a wise law professor who offered his students the following advice: "If you have the facts on your side, hammer them into the jury. If you have the law on your side, hammer it into the judge."

"And what if you have neither?" asked a young student.

"Then hammer on the table," he advised.

Whether you are talking to lawyers, police officers or judges, you need to choose your words carefully.

Questions to Ask *Before* You Hire an Attorney

"The minute you read something you can't understand, you can almost be sure it was written by lawyers."

—Will Rodgers, American wit, 1879–1935

Bennett Cerf, founder of Random House Publishing, liked to tell the story about an acquaintance of his who was sent a legal bill from an attorney for an informal chat they had at a cocktail party. A few days later, Cerf's miffed friend saw the attorney in an elevator and said, "Good day, sir." He then quickly added, "But mind you, I'm not asking your opinion about this. I'm merely stating a fact."

Most people, at one time or another, need legal advice, but finding the right attorney is not always easy.

"You need the right fit," says attorney Peter Fields, Esq., who specializes in entertainment and new media law for the New York firm of Phillips, Nizer, Benjamin Krim & Ballon. He added, "Don't be shy or afraid to ask questions."

When I asked Peter how to choose the right attorney, he suggested asking about the person's legal experience, fees and style of working *before* you make a decision.

• EXPERIENCE

As British philosopher Jeremy Bentham (1748–1832) wisely stated, "Lawyers are the only persons in whom ignorance of the law is not punished." Therefore, to avoid hiring an inexperienced attorney, ask him or her the following questions:

"How long have you been in practice?" (In general, the more experience the better, although new attorneys can be more conscientious.)

"Are you a sole practitioner or a partner or associate in a firm?" (Sole practitioners might give you more personalized attention, but partners and associates have more resources and backups if needed.)

"Do you specialize in a particular area of law?" (Be careful about attorneys—particularly sole practitioners—who say they can do everything. Attorneys who specialize usually provide better advice for issues that are more complex.)

"How much courtroom experience do you have?" (If you expect to go to court, make sure your attorney has had plenty of courtroom experience.)

"About what percentage of your recent cases are similar to mine?" (Asking the attorney this question will help you assess if he or she has enough current experience handling cases like yours.)

• FEES

When it comes to legal fees, discuss all the details up front. Here are the questions to ask:

"How will I be charged?"

"Is there a fee for the first consultation?"

"When are the fees due?"

"Are your fees negotiable?"

"How will I be charged for your expenses?"

"Can you estimate what your total fee will be?"

• WORKING RELATIONSHIP

Misunderstandings between attorneys and clients often begin when the relationship starts. Therefore, make sure you understand your obligations as a client and what you expect from your attorney in return.

"Will you be working on my case or will it be assigned to someone else?" (You have a right to know who will be working on your case.)

"Are you acquainted with the judges who hear cases like mine?" (Knowing a judge's preferences and style can make a big difference in the outcome of your case.)

"How will you keep me informed about the progress of my case?" (Establish your methods of communicating—telephone, e-mail, fax, letter or personal meetings—early on in your relationship. A major client complaint is lack of contact with their attorney.)

"What hours are you available for meetings?"

"Can you give me an idea of about how long it might take to resolve my case?" (Although you cannot hold an attorney to an exact date, based on similar cases, he or she should be able to give you an estimate of how long the matter will take to resolve.)

"What kinds of results have you had with cases like mine?" (Asking for the attorney's "batting average" for similar cases gives you an idea of the results you can expect.)

"Based on what you know about my case, what would be your strategy?" (Speak frankly about whether you are comfortable or uncomfortable with the attorney's approach to your case.)

"Can you give me an idea of what I might expect as a best outcome?" (Establishing reasonable expectations from the beginning of the relationship can prevent misunderstandings and friction later.)

"What could be the worst outcome?" (Knowing a worst-case scenario allows you to prepare for and deal with a negative outcome.)

"What expectations do you have of me as your client?" (Knowing and fulfilling your responsibilities will help your attorney do his or her job better.)

"What should I say to you if I'm concerned or not happy with the way you're handling my case?" (Having a complaint procedure in place can help avert a falling out between you and your attorney.)

"If we reach a point where the relationship is not working for either of us, how would we discontinue it?" (Establishing an amicable way to dissolve the client-attorney association shows that you have a professional approach to the relationship.)

You have learned the questions to ask in order to find an attorney who fits your needs. However, choosing the right attorney is only the first step if you want good legal advice. You will also need to know how to talk to your attorney.

Ten Biggest Mistakes Clients Make When Working with an Attorney

"For certain people, after fifty, litigation takes the place of sex."
—*Gore Vidal, American novelist, 1925–*

An attorney listened intently as his client claimed, "You may believe me or not, but I have not stated a word that is false, for I have been wedded to the truth from infancy."

"I'm sure," the seasoned attorney said, "but the question is, how long have you been divorced?"

Have you ever felt too embarrassed about a personal legal issue to tell an attorney the complete truth? If so, you have made one of the most common mistakes clients make when seeking legal advice. If you want your attorney to do the best job he or she can, avoid these common mistakes:

1. Remaining silent when you do not understand what your attorney says.

2. Making personal attacks or threatening your attorney with a malpractice lawsuit.

3. Arguing with your attorney about points of law.

4. Concealing the whole story or the complete truth, or telling your attorney what you think he or she wants to hear.

5. Not establishing clear communication channels at the beginning of the relationship.

6. Expecting "high drama" courtroom tactics like you see on television.

7. Not staying involved and up-to-date with your case.

How to Save Money on Legal Fees

Being well prepared for your attorney visits and discussions with your attorney can save you big bucks. Here are five simple ways to keep your attorney's "meter" from running up a huge legal bill:

- Prepare a short, written summary of your case.
- Bring copies of any relevant court documents.
- List all your questions and bring a copy to leave with your attorney.
- Bring a notebook and pen to take notes.
- Don't make small talk until after the meeting is officially over.

8. Not discussing options, reasonable outcomes and worst-case scenarios.

9. Expecting your attorney to devote all of his or her attention to your case.

10. Not taking careful notes during your conversations and meetings.

Five Strategies That (Maybe) Will Keep You from Getting a Traffic Ticket

"Warning! You want a warning? Okay, I'm warning you not to do that again or I'll give you another ticket."

—Unknown traffic cop

In his book, *Master of the Senate,* the author Robert Caro tells the story of how Lyndon Baines Johnson was driving near his Texas ranch and was pulled over by a patrolman for speeding. When the officer saw that the President of the United States was behind the wheel of the car, he gasped, "My God!" Without hesitating, the president drawled, "And don't you forget it."

Chances are, the traffic officer who pulled you over for a violation has heard every excuse in the book, so do not expect him or her to let you go because of some clever remark. On the other hand, if you talk to the officer in the right way, you may get out of the ticket altogether or perhaps only get written up for one violation instead of more. Here are some guidelines that will help make a positive impression on a traffic cop:

STRATEGY #1: Be respectful and polite

Police officers frequently say that the number-one problem they have with the drivers they stop is "bad attitude." Always be polite and use the title "Officer" when speaking. Treat men and women police officers equally, and never make any sexist remarks to the women officers.

STRATEGY #2: Remain in your car and put your hands on the steering wheel where the officer can see them

The first job of the police officer is to determine whether you pose a physical threat. A friendly, "Good morning (afternoon or evening), Officer" usually makes it clear that he or she has nothing to fear from you. When you hand over your driver's license and registration, offer a sheepish smile but admit nothing.

STRATEGY #3: Play dumb. Ask, "Did I do something wrong?"

There are times when a police officer may stop you because of a burnt-out taillight, of a smoking exhaust or to warn you to slow down or make complete stops at an intersections. It is in these "gray zones" where your behavior might convince the officer to let you off with a warning and not issue you a summons.

If the officer asks you, "Do you know why I stopped you?" or "Do you know how fast you were going?" look innocent and say:

"No, why?"

"I don't know why you stopped me."

"I have no idea."

"I thought I was obeying the traffic laws."

Note: Lying can erase any chance of you getting off with a warning.

STRATEGY #4: Offer an apology without admitting the violation

If your traffic violation is not too flagrant, an apology might get you off the hook. You can say, "My goodness, officer, I'm so sorry. I thought I was going the speed limit" or "Officer, I'm sorry. The glare made the light look yellow to me."

Note: Apologies can backfire. The officer might interpret your apology as, "I'm sorry I got caught."

STRATEGY #5: Plead for clemency before the officer checks you out on the computer

Before the officer leaves you and goes back to his or her patrol car to run your license, be sure to ask, "Do you think you could let me off with a warning this time instead of a ticket?" If you are lucky—and the officer is in a good mood—and if your license comes up clean, he or she may let you off with a warning.

Six Ways to Beat a Traffic Ticket

> *"You'll have to speak up because when you nod your head, the court reporter can't hear the rocks rattling."*
>
> *—From a deposition cited on reportercentral.com,*
> *the reference website for court reporters*

Israeli statesman Moshe Dayan (1915–1981) was easily recognized by his black eye patch. After getting a speeding ticket, he pleaded with the judge, "I have only one eye. What do you want me to watch—the speedometer or the road?"

Let's face it, if you got a traffic ticket, you probably deserved it. And

Twelve Things You Should Never Say to a Police Officer

Snappy remarks to traffic cops might get (canned) laughs on TV sitcoms, but they often can get you into more trouble if you have been pulled over for a moving violation. Here are a dozen thing *not* to say to a police officer who is considering giving you a ticket:

"I pay your salary."

"I'm a cop, too." (Who do you think you're kidding?)

"I'm good friends with one of your fellow officers."

"My radar detector wasn't plugged in."

"Don't you have anything better to do?"

"I was keeping up with the traffic."

"Your radar gun got the wrong car."

"Your radar gun must be calibrated wrong."

"I'm late for school (work, a hot date, etc.)."

"I'm about to get sick."

"I'm on my way to the hospital—my wife is having a baby."

"I have to find a toilet—desperately!"

"I'll see you in court."

if you are like most people, you'll bite the bullet, pony up the fine and cry when you see your insurance rates go up. However, if you feel the ticket was unjustified or that you have a good case, why not fight the ticket in court? Studies show that in many cases traffic judges will lower fines or dismiss tickets if you do the following:

1. REQUEST A COURT DATE

You can ask for a court date by certified mail or by going to the clerk's window at the courthouse. Once you have your date, take the time to prepare your case, collect all the necessary documents and practice your presentation.

2. BE ON TIME FOR YOUR COURT APPEARANCE AND HAVE YOUR DOCUMENTS IN ORDER

Allow plenty of time to get to the right courtroom and get your presentation ready. Judges are rarely lenient with disorganized people who are late.

3. HAVE A RESPECTFUL ATTITUDE

Show respect for the judge, the law, the court and the traffic officer. Never suggest that your ticket was the result of profiling, ineptness or anything else that may provoke the judge's ire.

4. PLEAD "NOT GUILTY"

Unless you have previously admitted to the violation and you are pleading "extenuating circumstances," you are, according to the law, "innocent until proven guilty." Now it is up to the traffic officer to provide the evidence, and the judge to determine whether it justified your ticket.

5. HAVE SEVERAL QUESTIONS READY TO ASK THE TRAFFIC OFFICER AND ATTACK THE EVIDENCE—NOT THE TRAFFIC OFFICER

Use questions to establish only the facts that may help you in your defense. Asking questions that you know the answer to will help you avoid testimony that might work against your case. The more you bring the validity of the evidence offered by the officer into question, the better your chances of beating the ticket or getting the fine reduced. Because many speeding tickets are based on radar, here are several questions that you can ask the officer in court about the radar gun:

"When was the radar gun was last tested for accuracy?" (You might question the radar gun's accuracy.)

"Where were you located when you used the radar gun?" (You might claim that the officer was parked on a curve or had his or her view obscured.)

"What was the distance between you and the car you registered on your radar gun, and what is the radar gun manufacturer's guideline for accurate readings?" (You might claim that the distance between the officer and you exceeded the manufacturer's guidelines.)

"How many other cars were in the exact area when you used the radar gun?" (You might claim that the reading was from another car.)

Remember that when it comes to fighting traffic tickets in court, you can win—but only if you show up, remain polite, do not try to be cute and present your evidence in a well-organized and respectful manner.

"The law does not concern itself about trifles."

—*Proverb*

You've learned that to talk successfully to lawyers, police officers and judges you need to respect their authority and present your arguments in an organized and businesslike manner. However, whether you win or lose your case, remember that your attorney will always collect his or her bill. Finally, remember that it's wise to be respectful when talking to lawyers, police officers and judges.

PART III

Words That Win in
Social Situations

CHAPTER FOURTEEN

Small Talk Secrets for
Socializing Success

"Don't bother telling people your troubles. Half of then don't care and the other half figure you probably had it coming."

—Josh Billings, American author, 1818–1885

In this chapter, you will learn:
• **Five steps to small talk** • **How to dodge personal questions** • **How to be a better listener** • **What to do if you become tongue-tied** • **Five steps for joining other conversations** • **What *not* to say when making small talk**

Have you ever wondered how some people can walk into a party or reception, chat with strangers and quickly make friends? One secret to socializing successfully is the ability to make small talk. Chatting with a stranger is much like dancing with a new partner. It takes a few minutes to get used to the other person's style, but before too long you can talk together as if you have known each other for years. People who know how to socialize well can make small talk with just about anyone, anywhere.

Five Steps to Small Talk

"One nice thing about egotists—they don't talk about other people."

—Lucille S. Harper

"Small talk" is an informal exchange of information, ideas and feelings that helps you build rapport with people you meet. Small talk allows strangers to quickly make connections and establish new relationships. There are five steps you can follow to make small talk—whether you are at a party, taking a walk in your neighborhood or browsing in a book-store.

STEP 1: Approach and say hello

Take the initiative and start a conversation with someone who looks approachable. How do you know if the person is open or closed to con-versation? It's easy if you look for body language signals like the ones below. A person who sends open body language signals is easier to ap-proach and converse with than one who has closed body language.

Body Language: The Good, the Bad and the Ugly

Open Body Language	Closed Body Language
√ Smiles	X Frowns, looks bored
√ Establishes eye contact	X Stares; looks away; gazes at ceiling, floor, magazines
√ Lets arms and hands move in a relaxed manner	X Wrapped arms around chest as if in a straight jacket
√ Walks around the room	X Stays in one place, leaves the room, sits alone in a big chair, remains at a distance away from others

---

STEP 2: Fish for topics with closed-ended questions

After you say hello to a stranger, it's time to "go fishing" for topics of conversation. Like the angler who casts out a line several times in hopes of a bite, you can toss out a few closed-ended (short-answer) questions and see how the other person responds.

What's Your "Hot Button"?

Hot buttons are topics that people love to talk about. Hot button topics include cars, playing softball, collecting rare records, bike riding, bird watching, chess, model building, painting, wine making or just about any other hobby or pursuit. When you discover a person's "hot button," you have struck conversational gold!

You can improve your chances of a positive response by looking for clues to the other person's areas of interest—jewelry, theme T-shirts, buttons, books, sports equipment, musical instruments or other items that you can ask about or comment on. Here are some examples:

To someone walking a dog, say, "What a great-looking dog. What kind is he?"

To someone reading a book on computers, say, "I see you are reading about computers. Are you taking a class?"

To someone carrying a guitar, say, "Do you play in a band?" or "What kind of music do you play?"

To someone carrying golf clubs, say, "Where do you play?"

To someone carrying take-out from a restaurant, say, "How's the food there?" or "What's for dinner?"

If the person responds enthusiastically to your fishing question, then continue to ask open-ended questions, make comments and share experiences of your own on that subject.

STEP 3: Reveal your topics of interests

To keep small talk going, you also need to disclose the topics that you are willing to talk about. If you do not tell, the other person may be too shy to ask. It is important to balance the amount of information you seek and the information you reveal so that at the end of the chat both of you have learned something about one another.

Here is what you can say to tell others your interests:

"I've been a member of this organization for years."

"I've moved here from . . . because it's close to the mountains. I love cross-country skiing."

"That's a coincidence. I studied . . . in school, too."

"I write computer programs for a software company, but my real passion is woodworking."

Caution: Don't tell your life story or reveal personal problems.

STEP 4: Listen for mutual interests

Keeping small talk going is easy if you actively listen for topics of mutual interest. An "active listener" picks up on and refers to key words—people, places, things and activities—that reveal how the person spends time, money and energy. The active listener asks follow-up questions and offers insightful comments and self-disclosures based on what he or she hears.

When someone brings up a topic that you are interested in, say so. That signals you are interested in what the other person is saying. For example, you can say:

"It's great meeting someone else who likes. . . ."

STEP 5: Change topics

There comes a time in every conversation when you need to change topics. Depending on your level of interest in a discussion, it could be after as little as five minutes or as much as a half-hour. How do you know when the time is right? Thirty seconds of silence is the most common signal that it is time to make a change. However, other signs include disagreements, overreactions or evasive answers. It is easy to change topics if you do the following:

- Listen carefully for any words, topics or references you can refer to when it comes time to change topics.

- When that time arrives, simply refer to any word, topic or reference that you want to talk about. To change topics, preface your question or comment with:

> "I heard you mention earlier that. . . ."

You can also change the subject by picking up on the word or topic—antique hunting, for example—and saying:

> "Antique hunting. That reminds me of a funny story."

A direct way to change the topic is to say:

> "I'd like to change the subject. There's something I've been meaning to ask (or tell) you."

Changing topics is how you can keep your small talk going strong. But it is also a way of helping you sidestep unwanted personal questions.

How to Dodge Personal Questions

If someone asks you a personal question that you do not want to answer, how can you respond without sounding rude? One answer is to sidestep the question. What constitutes a personal question varies. Most people consider inquiries concerning salary, how much certain things cost, sex, illness or personal problems as ill mannered, particularly if these questions come from new acquaintances. Here are examples of personal questions and how you can respond.

Personal question about money

"How much do you make?"
Answer: "More than (Not as much as) I'm worth."

"How much did it cost?"
Answer: "Less (More) than it should."

"How big was your raise?"
Answer: "I'd rather not say."

"How much did you inherit?"
Answer: "I prefer to keep that private."

Personal questions about your life at home

"So why did you get a divorce?"
Answer: "I don't really want to talk about it."

"How come I never see you with your spouse?"
Answer: "She (he) prefers to be elsewhere."

"What's the latest on your medical problem?"
Answer: "I'd rather not talk about that just now."

"Why don't you have any children?"
Answer: "Can't say, really."

To any ill-mannered question such as "Was your baby planned?" or "Did you have cosmetic surgery?"
Answer: "What? I can't believe you asked me that!"

If you keep your replies brief and polite, most people will accept your choice not to answer personal questions. However, if a nosy person persists, say, "I'd rather not talk about it." In most cases, it is up to you to change the subject to a more positive topic. You can say:

"Now, let me ask (tell) you about something else."

Once you know the five steps for making small talk, you are ready to tune up your listening skills.

How to Be a Better Listener

"A good listener is not someone who has nothing to say. A good listener is a good talker with a sore throat."
—Katherine Whitehorn, British journalist, 1926–

President Richard Nixon was shaking hands with a crowd of visitors to the White House when a little girl called out, "How's Smokey the Bear?" She was referring to a newly acquired bear at the Washington Zoo. Unable to make out the girl's words, Nixon turned to an aide for help. The aide whispered to him, "Smokey the Bear, Washington Zoo." A few minutes later, Nixon walked over to the girl, shook her hand and said, "How do you do, Miss Bear?"

Anyone can become a good listener. Here are several dos and don'ts that will immediately facilitate your ability to listen—from the boardroom to the bedroom and every room in between.

Do:

- Listen for and remember details and main ideas.

- Listen "between the lines" for feelings and implied statements.

- Let others complete their thoughts.

- Listen for "hot buttons"—topics of high interest.

- Share your interest in something the person said.

- Paraphrase main ideas.

- Acknowledge the speaker's feelings.

- Ask some clarification questions.

- Ask more about a high-interest topic.

Don't:

- Interrupt or finish a person's sentences.

- Avoid eye contact as someone talks to you.

- Look at your watch or fidget as the other person speaks.

- Change topics before the person has finished sharing his or her views.

- Ask too many closed-ended questions in a row.

- Only listen for mistakes or contradictions.

- Shake your head before he or she finishes.

- Assume a nod of the head means understanding or agreement.

Gracious listening is one of the secrets to making small talk. But did you know it is also the key to knowing what to say when your tongue turns into a big knot?

What to Say When You Become Tongue-Tied

Have you ever been in a conversation and meant to say one thing, but instead you jumbled your words or felt your mind go blank? Everyone— even good conversationalists—occasionally experience that embarrassing situation when the brain goes numb and the tongue becomes tied.

The problem often stems from focusing inward, worrying too much, or trying too hard to be clever or to sound knowledgeable. These pitfalls can leave you speechless. Here are several reasons why you might lose your train of thought or become tongue-tied and what you can do and say to get the words flowing again.

Pitfall: You are thinking about what to say instead of listening.

What to do: Refocus your attention to the other person. Say:

"I'm sorry, I missed what you just said. Could you run that by me again?"

Pitfall: You are nervous and worried that you will say something stupid or inappropriate, so you freeze up.

What to do: Encourage the other person to talk by asking an open-ended question. Let your curiosity guide you. Say:

"What made you decide to . . . ?"

Pitfall: You put yourself down with demeaning self-talk so you become afraid to open your mouth.

What to do: Replace negative self-talk with these three affirmations: STOP! LOOK! LISTEN! Say:

"Stop putting yourself down."

"Look and pay attention to what he (or she) is saying."

"Listen and respond to what you hear."

Pitfall: You wonder if the other person will like you.

What to do: Show genuine interest in him or her. Say:

"I'm glad we are getting a chance to chat."

Pitfall: You think you are boring.

What to do: Share your passions and interests and see how the other person responds. You never know—he or she may be interested in what interests you. Say:

"I did something really fun last weekend."

"I've just recently become interested in. . . ."

What if the other person asks you a question and you freeze up? Don't worry. Take a deep breath, exhale and laugh. Then say something silly. For example:

"Forgive me, I'm having a senior moment."

Now you know what to do if your mind goes blank, if you jumbled your words or if your tongue becomes tied. The next goal is to join other conversations—and the easiest way to do that is to look around and see who is talking.

Five Steps for Joining Other Conversations

"The cocktail party is designed for multiple, quick social encounters rather than prolonged conversations. It may be argued that that makes the event rude by nature."

—Judith Martin (Miss Manners), American etiquette expert

You can use your small talk skills to approach and join people who are already engaged in conversation. Joining them is far easier than most people think. Don't assume that people around the room who are talking enthusiastically are old friends. As likely as not, they just met minutes ago. Here are the five simple steps to joining in the fun.

STEP 1: Look for a group that you think is open to newcomers and has some people you want to meet.

STEP 2: Move to within three to five feet, or "overhearing distance." Listen to make sure the conversation interests you.

STEP 3: Show you are listening by establishing eye contact with the speakers.

STEP 4: React to what you hear. Use gestures, such as smiling, nodding and raising your eyebrows.

STEP 5: When there is a pause, ask an easy-to-answer question based on what you hear. Or say:

"Do you mind if I join you?"

Your ability to make small talk can help you become a social success, as long as you do not put your foot in your mouth. By keeping the conversation light and fun, you will create a positive and lasting impression.

What *Not* to Say When Making Small Talk

Small talk is an effective way to build rapport—if you don't make these mistakes:

Don't:

- Criticize others with whom you disagree.

- Argue about sex, politics or religion.

- Focus on negative subjects, such as crime, etc.

- Bring up personal problems at work or home.

- Reveal medical problems or recent operations.

- Go on about pet peeves or complaints.

- Correct other people's grammatical mistakes.

- Quibble over minor differences or facts.

- Ask personal questions or reveal family secrets.

- Be a know-it-all.

- Tell off-color jokes to new acquaintances.

- Gossip about people you know.

"The real art of conversation is not only to say the right thing in the right place but to leave unsaid the wrong thing at the tempting place."
—*Dorothy Nevill, British hostess*

Making small talk is easy if you prepare topics of conversation for the event. When you listen, you make others feel important and know what to say next. If you become tongue-tied, don't worry—take another breath, smile and begin again. Joining others in conversation is easy— just say, "May I join you?"

CHAPTER FIFTEEN

Building Better Ties with Your Neighbors

"I've never really adapted myself to life here in Los Angeles. I've been here eleven years and my watch is still on New York time."
—Mel Brooks, American comedian, 1926–

In this chapter, you will learn:
• **Four things you can do to welcome new neighbors** • **Six tips when you move into a new neighborhood** • **Twelve rude things that really annoy neighbors** • **How to complain to a neighbor** • **How to smooth the feathers of an offended neighbor**

Soon after a friend of mine moved into a house in a quiet Seattle neighborhood, she heard a knock at the door. It was an older man standing on her front porch. He introduced himself as her neighbor and held out a bowl of fresh raspberries from his garden. This warm gesture made my friend feel welcome to the neighborhood and set the tone for her relationship with this friendly neighbor.

Four Things You Can Do to Welcome New Neighbors

Moving into a new neighborhood is always a little scary. What are the neighbors like, and will they be friendly? My friend's experience illustrates the positive impact that even a small gift can make on a new neighbor.

Respect Your New Neighbor's Privacy

Some people might not want to disclose too much about themselves to strangers—even if they live right next door. If you sense that your new neighbor is a "private person," do not ask too many questions or you might give the impression of being a snoop or meddler.

Most newcomers agree that the sooner they meet their neighbors, the more comfortable they are living in their new home. Here are four ways to make new neighbors feel welcome:

1. OFFER A WARM WELCOME YOUR NEW NEIGHBOR

Let's face it, many newcomers to a street or apartment building feel too shy or embarrassed to introduce themselves to their neighbors—that's why residents often remain relative strangers for months. However, a warm welcome makes newcomers feel comfortable because someone has taken the initiative to break the ice and exchange names.

To welcome someone to your neighborhood, say:

"How do you do. I'm. . . . I live across the street. I just wanted to welcome you to the neighborhood."

"Hi, My name is. . . . I know you just moved into the apartment upstairs, so we're neighbors. I live on the first floor. What's your name?"

2. OFFER ASSISTANCE

Do you remember how much work it was the last time you moved into a new home? Carrying boxes, unloading building materials, painting, cleaning, repairing—the list goes on and on. Offering to help your new neighbors creates instant goodwill. Don't go overboard—a simple offer such as lending a tool or helping unload supplies will do. By offering your help, you are showing that you know how to be a good neighbor.

Here is what you can say:

> "Let me know if you ever need any help."

> "I'm afraid my back is not up to any heavy lifting, but I'm handy with. . . ."

3. SHOW A WILLINGNESS TO HAVE A GOOD RELATIONSHIP

It takes more than good fences to make good neighbors, at least in today's loud world of bass-thumping stereos, squealing car alarms, droning leaf-blowers, grinding power saws and countless other noisy irritations. As a result, neighbors—new and old—need to be considerate, sensitive and tolerant of one another. Therefore, a few well-chosen words to a new neighbor can head off minor irritations before they grow into major problems. Say:

> "Our kids can get pretty loud sometimes when they are playing basketball in the backyard. If they get too obnoxious, just tell them to pipe down."

> "I just wanted to let you know that we're beginning a kitchen renovation soon, and I'm sure it's going to be a bit loud. I'll do my best to keep the noise down, but if I disturb you too much, be sure to let me know."

4. EXTEND AN INVITATION TO A NEIGHBORHOOD GET TOGETHER

Socializing with your neighbors is a great way to get to know one another. Some neighbors hold regular parties, picnics, card games, barbecues, yard sales or other informal get-togethers. Extending an invitation to a new neighbor sends the clear signal that you want to be friendly. You can send a written invitation or simply say something like:

> "We're having a little party next Saturday afternoon, and we're hoping that you would like to come. Some of the neighbors will be there, so you'll know a few people. Would you like to join us?"

"Would you like to attend our next Neighborhood Block Association meeting? It's a good opportunity to meet others who live on the block."

Six Tips When You Move into a New Neighborhood

"Suburbia is where the developer bulldozes out the trees and then names the streets after them."

—Bill Vaughan, American author, 1915–1977

In a town just north of New York City, new homeowners moved into their house with a big tree-filled yard and promptly cut down several 150-year-old trees. The neighbors were outraged. "I don't think anybody should be allowed to cut down big trees, especially if they're over a hundred years old," another grumbled. "They've ruined our neighborhood."

Fitting into a neighborhood can be tricky, especially if many of the people there are longtime residents. If you want to avoid rubbing your neighbors the wrong way, consider these six tips when you move into a new neighborhood.

TIP #1: Ask the former owner or occupant to introduce you to a few of the neighbors

Being introduced to a few of your new neighbors and exchanging names is the easiest way to break the ice. You probably will not spend more than a few minutes chatting during this initial encounter, but that is enough time to make a positive first impression and to set the relationship off on the right direction. Just ask a former occupant to introduce you:

"Would you introduce me to a few of your neighbors?"

TIP #2: Introduce yourself to the next-door neighbors

Friendly neighbors will knock on your door, introduce themselves and welcome you to the block or building. However, if after a few days you still have not met your next-door neighbors, then take the initiative and introduce yourself. You can say:

"Hello, I'm your new neighbor. My name is. . . ."

TIP #3: Adapt to the "neighborhood culture"

Being accepted as the new kid on the block is easier if you adopt a "When in Rome, do as the Romans" philosophy of fitting in to your neighborhood. For example, if the street is always quiet before 9 A.M. on Sundays, wait until later in the day to complete noisy chores. Or if longtime residents have noisy kids, it's best to just grin and bear it—until you have lived there a while.

TIP #4: Compliment your neighbors on their homes

Most people take pride in their homes, so a compliment is a great way to break the ice and introduce yourself. For example, you can say:

"What a beautiful garden! It really makes the block sparkle. By the way, I live on the next street. My name is. . . ."

TIP #5: Take part in neighborhood-sponsored activities

Although some neighborhoods have more social activities than others, you probably can find several opportunities to socialize with your neighbors. Perhaps the most common events are neighborhood get-togethers at holidays, open houses, block parties or sporting-event parties like the Super Bowl or World Series. Joining in on the fun shows that you want to get to know your neighbors and that you want to be included in the social life of where you live.

When you are invited to a neighborhood event, be sure to say how pleased and you are. You can say something like:

"Thanks for inviting me to your. . . . I'll definitely be there! What can I bring?"

If you have to decline, still show your appreciation for the invitation. Add a brief explanation of why you cannot attend. For example, you might say something like:

"I appreciate you thinking of me, but I've got other plans for that day (evening). I'd love to come next time, so please be sure ask me again."

TIP #6: Over time, meet as many of your neighbors as you can.

Although you'll probably meet your next-door neighbors and the people living across the street from you soon after you move in, it might take longer to make contact with other people living on your block or in your building. Don't worry if after a few weeks or even months you still haven't met all your neighbors. Eventually, you will have the opportunity to smile, say hello and introduce yourself. Say:

"Hi, I moved to the neighborhood a few months ago. I've been meaning to introduce myself. My name's. . . ."

Twelve Rude Things That Really Annoy Neighbors

"Why be disagreeable, when with a little effort you can be impossible?"
—Douglas Woodruff, British writer, 1897–1978

Businessman Franklin P. Jones once said, "Nothing makes you more tolerant of a neighbor's noisy party than being there." However, you can really offend your neighbors by doing any of the following:

1. Frequently hosting loud parties

2. Playing loud music late at night

3. Allowing overgrown shrubs or trees to extend over property lines or block others' views

4. Allowing children to play loudly at all hours

5. Walking with noisy shoes on bare apartment floors

6. Allowing your friends to use neighbors' parking spaces

7. Allowing dogs to use neighbors' lawns as a toilet, bark, or roam unaccompanied

8. Doing loud repair work or renovations at night

9. Mowing lawns early on weekends

10. Vacuuming or using power tools late at night

11. Not returning borrowed tools

12. Parking in a another tenant's parking space

How to Complain to a Neighbor

"Keeping up with the Jones's was a full-time job with my mother and father. It wasn't until many years later when I lived alone that I realized how much cheaper it was to drag the Jones' down to my level."
—Quentin Crisp, British author, 1910–1999

Yes, I accept that noise is part of city life, but incessant car alarms drive me crazy! As a result, I take action when someone's alarm keeps going off in the middle of the day or at night. I write this brief note and place it under the offending car's windshield wiper.

Dear Neighbor,
Did you know that your car alarm has been going off every hour or so—all night (or day) long? The loud honking and sirens make it hard for us to sleep (or work). Please do all of us a favor and fix it. Everyone in the neighborhood will sure appreciate it.
Thanks,
Your neighbors

Surprisingly, a simple, polite note like this usually embarrasses the offending neighbor enough to get the problem fixed. If a neighbor's behavior bothers you, first ask yourself if the annoyance is important and frequent enough to make a fuss about. If you determine that it is, follow this four-step strategy to complain to a neighbor—and get satisfactory results.

STEP 1: Calmly and simply state the problem

Your neighbor might not even know that his or her behavior has caused you a problem until you bring it up. Chances are, if your relationship is good, your neighbor will do his or her best to correct the situation. Be specific. Vague complaints rarely get resolved. Do not make exaggerated generalizations like, "I'm going crazy!" or "It is making my life hell!"

STEP 2: Describe how the problem affects you

Explain how your neighbor's behavior directly affects you, and do not forget to include several specific examples. By personalizing the problem, your neighbor might be more understanding and willing to make some adjustments.

STEP 3: Suggest a solution

Just complaining about a problem is rarely enough to get results—you need to take it a step further and say how you want the issue resolved. Because some problems may be easier or less expensive for your neighbor to fix than others, ask yourself if your request is reasonable. Is it easy or difficult? Cheap or expensive? Can you compromise?

STEP 4: Express your appreciation

It is amazing how quickly some people forget their good manners when they become annoyed with a neighbor. If you want to avoid a backlash after complaining to a neighbor, do not forget to express your gratitude with "magic words" such as "please" . . . "thank you" . . . "I appreciate it" . . . "thanks for your cooperation" . . . "let's work things out."
    In addition to following these four steps, your chances of getting some

satisfaction from your neighbor largely depend upon you and your neighbor's:

- Ability to speak directly with respect and tact.

- Prior relationship and your attitude toward each other.

- Desire to maintain goodwill.

- Willingness to accept a reasonable resolution.

Here is an example of how to use this four-step approach.

PROBLEM: LOUD MUSIC LATE AT NIGHT

Step 1: State the problem
"Maybe you didn't realize how thin the walls are in this building, but the volume at which you play your stereo makes it sound like it's in my bedroom, and that's a real problem for me."

Step 2: How the problem affects you
"It's been so loud over the last few days that I haven't been able to sleep until after you turned it off, and that was well past 1 A.M. That really makes it tough on me, especially because I have to get up very early every morning."

Step 3: Suggest a solution
"I have no argument with your right to play music, but could you do me a favor and turn down the volume some or use earphones, especially after 10 o'clock?"

Step 4: Express your appreciation
"I really appreciate you doing me this favor."

How to Smooth the Feathers of an Offended Neighbor

Even good neighbors can cause offense from time to time. However, a real problem can be averted through speedy action. The sooner you take responsibility for your actions, apologize and repair any damage, the better. Here is how to make things right when you have offended a neighbor.

APOLOGIZE WITHOUT BEATING AROUND THE BUSH

The first step in righting a wrong is to apologize without blaming someone else or making excuses. Be direct and say something like:

> "I apologize for . . . (my dog using your lawn as a latrine, parking in your spot, etc.)."

> "I'm really sorry for any inconvenience I caused you."

> "I'm sorry about the damaged window (sidewalk, etc.)."

ACKNOWLEDGE YOUR NEIGHBOR'S RIGHT TO BE ANGRY

When your neighbor is angry with you, restate the reason he or she has given you why he or she is angry. This shows you are listening and understand why he or she is upset. This simple action makes your apology more genuine and acceptable. Say:

> "I'd be upset, too, if someone . . . (broke my window, kept me up half the night, etc.)."

> "I don't blame you one bit for being angry when my kid's basketball squashed the plants."

THANK YOUR NEIGHBOR FOR BRINGING A PROBLEM TO YOUR ATTENTION

If your neighbor brings up a problem caused by you or your family that you were unaware of, express your thanks for bringing it to your attention. You can say:

> "I appreciate you letting me know that. . . . I had no idea it was causing you a problem."

"How embarrassing! I didn't realize that I had broken the tool (camera, etc.) that I borrowed from you."

"I wasn't aware that my practicing piano (vacuuming, etc.) was so loud that it kept you awake. Sorry."

OFFER TO TAKE CORRECTIVE ACTION

After you have apologized, acknowledged your neighbor's right to complain and thanked him or her for bringing a problem to your attention, it is time for you act. If you minimize the problem or delay resolving the issue, you can not only damage your relationship with your neighbor, but also cause long-lasting bad will.

To avoid further anger or a neighborhood feud, tell your neighbor something like:

"I really want to make things right between us, so I'd like to replace the window (repair the fence, etc.)."

"I'm embarrassed that you needed to bring . . . to my attention. I promise it won't happen again. I want to pay for the repair."

"I'll personally take care of the problem today."

"No one is rich enough to do without his neighbors."
                                                      —*Proverb*

Staying on good terms with your neighbors is not always easy, but it is worth the effort. It takes good communication skills, assertiveness and a desire to get along. The American writer Eric Hoffer (1902–) may have described the challenge of fitting into a neighborhood best when he wrote, "It is easier to love humanity as a whole than to love one's neighbor."

CHAPTER SIXTEEN

How to Make and Keep
Friends for Life

"When the chips are not exactly down but scattered about, you discover who your real friends are."

—Richard Burton, British actor, 1925–1984

In this chapter, you will learn
• **Four steps to friendships** • **Fourteen sure-fire ways to *lose* friends** • **How to reconnect old friendships** • **Eight situations with friends that call for tactful words** • **Seven golden rules of friendships**

Every spring I have met with ten school friends for a three-day reunion. Some of us became friends in elementary school, others in junior high and high school. We called ourselves the Eastside Boys, and we were infamous for our pranks and great parties. Today, more than 40 years later, we still have a great time getting together, playing poker, and talking about the good old days.

What makes us special is that we have stayed in regular contact for so many years. When I talk to others about my friendships with the Eastside Boys, most are surprised. Many tell me that they have completely lost touch with their friends from childhood, high school or college. They think it is great that my friends and I have remained in contact. And the Eastsiders agree—our long friendships mean a lot.

Four Steps to Friendship

"If you want a friend in Washington, get a dog."
—Harry Truman, thirty-third U.S. president, 1884–1972

Making friends is a lifelong proposition. You can make friends with just about anyone at any time in your life if you are willing to spend some time getting to know each other. Most people who become friends build their relationship on a foundation of familiarity, common interests, experiences and a shared sense of humor. You can build friendships with people you meet through these four steps.

STEP 1: Build familiarity

Familiarity plants the seeds of friendship. When you see and chat regularly with people where you live, work, worship and play, you will get a sense of the people whose company you enjoy and whose interests you share. Once you have established rapport with these people, friendships can begin and develop.

STEP 2: Spend informal time together

Once you have chatted with someone enough to know that you share common interests and that you enjoy each other's company, suggest a social outing together. Keep your first few times together informal and short. Here are a few good ways for new friends to spend time together.

- Go out for coffee, share a meal or get a drink.
- Go to a movie, concert, play or sporting event.
- Take a walk, go jogging together or go on a bike ride.
- Go to a museum or attend a book signing.
- Attend a party or networking event.

When you get together with your new friend, your objectives are to have fun and learn more about one another. Be sure to include *some* ritual information—basic personal background and interesting facts. A *balanced* exchange of ritual information is how you will get to know each other better, build rapport and establish trust. Ritual information includes:

- Where you are from

- Where you live

- What you do for a living

- If you are married or single

- When you came to the area where you now live

- Some of your special interests

- Some family background

Keep the conversation balanced so that neither of you talks too much, and make sure any self-disclosures are not overly personal. In other words, do not tell your life story or reveal any of your deepest, darkest secrets—at least not until you get to know your new friend better. Avoid the following topics as well—at least until you get to know the person a little better:

- Personal problems, including health, financial or substance abuse (unless the situation you are in relates to these issues; i.e., Alcoholics Anonymous, or support group, etc.)

- Politics (unless you know the person shares your views or the situation you are in relates to or is politically oriented; i.e., political rally, community discussion group, etc.)

- Religion (unless you know the person shares your beliefs or the situation you are in relates to a religious event or activity; i.e., dance, fund-raiser, etc.)

- Personal details about past relationships

Listen carefully and remember what your new friend tells you. Showing interest and being a good listener are major components of a good friendship, along with self-disclosure. Talking about things that are important to you provides a platform upon which your friendship will develop.

Questions you can ask:
"Can you tell me a little about where you are from?"

"What made you decide to move here?"

"How did you end up working (volunteering, etc.) here?"

"How did you become interested in . . . ?"

Information you can reveal:
"I grew up in . . . and moved here in. . . ."

"I got my degree in . . . but decided that I wanted to try a variety of jobs before settling into a career."

"To pay the rent I . . . but my real dream is. . . ."

Step 3: Spend extended time together
As you become better friends, you will want to spend more time together. Extended time might include an evening, a day or maybe even a weekend. Again, the objectives are to have fun, enjoy each other's company, and get to know one another better. The extended time allows you both to be yourselves and continue building rapport and trust. Here are a few ways you can spend extended time together:

- Attend a daylong event such as a conference, music festival, hike and picnic, walking tour, etc.

- Go on a day trip antique hunting, apple picking, shopping or exploring a new place or town.

- Attend an out-of-town conference, resort spa, etc.

- Go camping or on a trip for the weekend.

Thinking About Vacationing with a Friend?

When it comes to spending more than a day together, follow your instincts and avoid any hasty decisions. Be sure you have spent enough time together on a daily basis before you commit to a weekend get-away or longer vacation together. Discuss your travel styles and come to some agreement before you agree to vacation together. For example, you might say:

"I wish I could afford to stay in a first-class hotel, but most are too expensive. I get a moderately priced room in a clean hotel in a good location. What kind of rooms do you usually get when you travel?"

"I like to get up early and explore the area when I'm on vacation. How about you?"

"I describe my travel style as slow. I prefer spending time and getting to know the flavor of a place rather than trying to cover too much territory. How would you best describe your travel style?"

• Plan a short vacation together or with other friends—but make sure that you have compatible travel styles.

STEP 3: Build deeper bonds by sharing personal information and meaningful experiences

True friendship allows people to confide in one another with the understanding that any revelations will be held in confidence and will be accepted without judgment. As mutual trust grows, discussing personal information with a friend becomes less risky. As the friendship deepens, so do the revelations and vulnerability. When you listen to a friend, avoid making criticizing or patronizing remarks.

At the same time, do not overburden your new friend with your troubles or demand too much sympathy or support. A "broken winger" (someone who constantly talks about and seeks help for his or her personal problems) rarely keeps new friends for long.

Fifteen Sure-Fire Ways to Lose Friends

"Whenever a friend succeeds, a little something in me dies."
—Gore Vidal, American writer, 1925–

Whether your friendship grows quickly or develops slowly over time, never take your friends for granted or they may not stick around. Here are fifteen sure-fire ways to lose friends.

1. Violating trust
2. Talking only about yourself
3. Talking or gossiping behind a friend's back
4. Revealing a friend's secret
5. Criticizing weight, appearance or other relationships
6. Asking for too many favors and never reciprocating
7. Being unavailable
8. Dropping your friend for another friend or romantic interest
9. Not apologizing for inappropriate or insensitive behavior
10. Stealing a boyfriend, girlfriend or date
11. Being unpredictable
12. Not respecting a friend's opinion
13. Acting rude or making snide remarks
14. Being chronically late
15. Not showing up for a get-together without calling

You always have the potential to make new friendships if you make sure they are based on common interests, shared experiences and mutual respect.

How to Reconnect Old Friendships

"It's the friends you can call at 4 A.M. that matter."
—Marlene Dietrich, German singer and actress, 1901–1992

When the recorded music of the Glen Miller and Count Basie bands began to play at Washington High School's fiftieth class reunion, the dance floor burst with activity. One man and his wife—both a few pounds heavier and a bit slower than they were when they graduated—put on a show with their version of Ginger Rodgers and Fred Astaire dancing to "Waltz in Swing Time."

As the couple glided by, a woman sitting on the sidelines chirped, "Hey Jack, if I'd known you were going to turn out such a good dancer, I never would have said no when you asked me to the senior prom!"

ATTEND REUNIONS

Whether it has been ten, fifteen, twenty-five or even fifty years since you attended summer camp or graduated from high school, attending reunions are a great way to reconnect with old friends and make new ones, too. Some high schools have annual golf reunions, dances, picnics or other informal get-togethers for their alumni. There are plenty of reasons for attending reunions other than just reliving the "good old days." Here are a few:

- Reconnect with a former school sweetheart.

- See what happened to the guy or gal "who got away."

- Reconnect with friends who drifted away.

- Become friendly with classmates you barely knew.

- Find out what classmates did with their lives.

- Find old friends who may be living nearby.

- Establish new business and personal relationships.

- See old teachers and tell them how much they meant to you.

OTHER PLACES TO RECONNECT WITH OLD FRIENDS

Here are some other places to connect with old friends:

- Do a people search on the Internet in the city or area where you grew up or met your old friends.

- Visit your old neighborhood. You might be surprised how many of your old buddies still live in the area.

- Talk to mutual friends who might know the whereabouts of old acquaintances.

HOW TO TALK TO FRIENDS YOU HAVEN'T SEEN IN YEARS

"What have you been doing all these years?" is probably the most frequently asked question at reunions, so it is wise to have a *short* reply ready. You might say:

"I've been living in . . . for the last . . . years, working as a. . . . I'm . . . (married, single, divorced, widowed) with . . . kids ages. . . . Now I'm living in . . . with my two kids. What about you?"

"I'm single now. I live with . . . (alone, my kids, pets, etc.) and work for (spend time). . . . What about you?"

HANDLING QUESTIONS ABOUT DIVORCE AND DEATH

Questions about spouses or significant others inevitably come up during these catch-up chats with old friends. Assuming that an old friend is still married or in a relationship can lead to an embarrassing or distressing moment for both people. To tactfully find out about your old friend's relationship status you can ask:

"Are you still married?"

"Did you ever marry?" (Never ask, "Why not?")

"Do you live alone or with someone?"

If you are divorced, you might be tempted to reveal the more personal details of your breakup, but do not do it—at least not now. Instead, be direct, brief and pleasant by avoiding nasty comments. You can say something like:

> "I split up with . . . years ago. It was for the best."

> "Lee and I decided it was better for all of us to live our lives apart. The kids live with each of us six months of the year."

> "I've been divorced for several years."

When someone tells you of his or her divorce, never congratulate the person or pry. It is best to move the conversation to, hopefully, a more pleasant subject. For example, you can say:

> "Ah, and so how is your wonderful daughter doing? Is she still as precocious as I remember?"

> "I see. So what else is going on with you?"

If someone in your family has died you can say:

> "Unfortunately, . . . died last year."

> "I am sad to say that my . . . died . . . years ago."

If someone tells you about a death in the family it is best to say, "I am so sorry." If you knew the person, say something positive or nice about him or her and avoid questions about the details of the death.

PATCH UP A BROKEN FRIENDSHIP

Even good friends can get into disagreements that can cause a breach in their friendship. If that happens, it might take time for tempers to calm down. However, the sooner you take the initiative and suggest reconciliation with your friend, the more likely it is to happen. To patch up a broken friendship, you need to tell your friend that you value the friendship and want to get it back on track.

You can say it in a letter, in an e-mail or on the telephone. Keep in mind that you might need to apologize for a breach of confidence or some other indiscretion that led to the argument in the first place. Even if you feel that your friend owes you an apology, you might need to be the one to hold out the olive branch. Here is what you can say to patch up a quarrel with a friend:

"I'm really sorry we had that argument yesterday. You know how worked up I can get sometimes, but that's no excuse. What I said to you really hurt your feelings and I apologize. I was out of line, and it just plain wrong of me to say what I did to you. I want you to know that I value our friendship, and I hope that you'll forgive me."

"I know we've had our differences, but let's get back to being friends again. I'm sure we both said things that we regret, but I'm willing to let bygones be bygones, if you are."

Here are three other easy ways to reestablish contact:

- Write a personal letter.

- Send an e-mail.

- Pick up the telephone.

Unlike e-mails and traditional letters, telephone conversations take place in "real time" so you need to be ready to chat when the person answers. (See Chapter 14 for tips on making small talk.) Always begin all your telephone conversations by introducing yourself. Say something like:

"Hello, my name is. . . . I'm trying to reach an old high school class-mate (roommate, Army buddy, etc.) of mine,. . . Are you by any chance him (or her)?"

If the person says yes, then say:

"That's great! How are you? Do you have a few minutes to chat, or can I call you back at a more convenient time?"

You might need to remind the person who you are. After all, memories fade and without being able to see you, it might be difficult to place your name with a face. For example, you might say:

"I was the skinny guy who sat behind you in senior English and always teased you. By the way, sorry about that."

"We played on the same softball team in high school. I played catcher."

"We sat next to each other in the band. I played saxophone—in fact, I still do. Do you still play clarinet?"

Again, focus on positive events, not bad health, tragedies or personal problems. Do not expect your first conversation to be more than a few minutes. If the conversation goes well, exchange telephone numbers and e-mail addresses, and say:

"I'd love to stay in touch, if that's okay with you. Can I give you my telephone number and e-mail? And I'd like to get yours, too."

Reconnecting with old friends is like seeing your favorite movie for the umpteenth time—it's fun, entertaining and rewarding all over again. However, whether your friendship is new, rekindled or ongoing, sensitive topics and issues will come up that will require you to speak with tact.

Eight Situations with Friends That Call for Tactful Words

"The true essence of friendships is to make allowances for another's little lapses."

—David Storey, British novelist and playwright, 1933–

If a friend takes your friendship for granted or speaks to you in a nasty, self-centered or just thoughtless way, you might be tempted to answer with a harsh rebuke or snappy comeback—if you can think of one on the spot. Although a clever or cutting retort may make you feel better at the time, it can quickly escalate into an argument.

It is better to take the higher ground and claim to be injured by your friend's tactless comments than to hurl a spear in anger and risk impaling a good friendship.

- To a friend who complains say:

  "What can you do to change the situation?"
  "What are your options?"
  "Is there anything I can do to help?"

- To a friend who is late say:

  "Please be early. Then you'll be on time."
  "If you know you're running late, please call me. Here is my cell phone number in case you don't have it."

- To a friend who is super-critical, say:

  "Perhaps it's not perfect, but I like it anyway."

- To a friend who badmouths your other friends, spouse or lover, say:

  "I'm sure you have your reasons for saying that, but I don't really want to know what they are."

- To a friend who has hurt your feelings, say:

  "I wish you hadn't said that."

- To a friend who fails to promptly return your telephone calls, use a little bit of humor and say:

  "I'd appreciate it if you'd return my calls."

Sometimes you may encourage a tardy friend to return your calls more promptly. For example, you might say:

  "Gee, I wish you had called me back sooner. I had a couple of extra free tickets to a concert. . . ."

- To a friend who asks for too many favors, be sympathetic, but firm. You can say:

Advice for Friends with Alcohol or Drug Abuse Problems

What can you say that will help a friend who has a drinking or drug problem that is affecting your friendship? Most recovering alcoholics and drug abusers agree that chides or threats from friends rarely do more than cause resentment and alienation.

According to Al-Anon, a nonprofit organization that offers hope and help for families and friends of alcoholics, The best advice you can offer a friend who has a substance abuse problem is to say:

"Talk to someone who can help you."

"I think you need to get some professional help."

"I'm you're friend and that's why I'm saying this. You have a drinking (drug) problem and need help."

"I'm concerned about your drinking (drug use)."

"I'm sorry, but I can't help you any more than I already am."

- To a friend who offers you too much unsolicited advice, you can say:

"Thank you. I'll think about it."

"I know you're just trying to help, but I'll deal with it in my own way."

Seven Golden Rules of Friendships

At times, maintaining a friendship can be difficult—it requires patience, attention and choosing the right words, but the benefits of true friendship far outweigh the demands. Here are seven sure-fire rules to win friends and keep them for life.

RULE #1: True friends are there when they are needed.

RULE #2: True friends accept one another for who they are.

RULE #3: True friends have an emotional stake in their friends' lives.

RULE #4: True friends do not base their relationship on selfish motives.

RULE #5: True friends remain loyal.

RULE #6: True friends do not drop old friends for new ones.

RULE #7: True friends know: "To have a friend you must be a friend."

"Your friend is the man who knows all about you, and still likes you."
—*Elbert Hubbard, American writer, 1856–1915*

Making and keeping friends for life happens when you put effort into your relationships. Spend enjoyable time with your new friends, and re-connect with your old friends. Violating trust, showing little interest or being overcritical will cause you to lose friends. Most friends, at one time or another, need to know that you are there for them, so don't let them down.

CHAPTER SEVENTEEN

Surviving and Thriving on a First Date

"Love's like the measles—all the worse when it comes late in life."
—Douglas W. Jerrold, British dramatist, 1803–1857

In this chapter, you'll learn:
• **Where to find dates** • **Five ways to attract the opposite sex** • **How to ask for a date** • **How to handle a rejection** • **Four tips for first dates** • **How to end a first date**

The ritual of dating can be exciting, scary, frustrating, and sometimes even painful—especially if you are inexperienced, have had a few broken relationships or have been recently divorced or widowed. How do you ask for a date? What should you do on a first date? And finally, how do you find the right person for a more serious relationship?

Where to Find Dates

"I have such bad vision I can date anybody."
—Gary Shandling, American comedian, 1949–

There are many ways to find a date. Well-meaning relatives or friends often say, "I know someone you'd just love! Why don't go out and see what happens?" Although most blind dates are doomed from the start, some do lead to romance. Other places to find potential dates include:

- Set up a date with someone you have just met.

  The advantage of dating a new acquaintance is that you know what each other looks like, you have chatted some and you have made an acceptable first impression.

- Go out with someone you have already spent time with or know but have never officially dated.

  There are two advantages of asking someone you already know. One is that you are aware of your common interests and feel comfortable spending time together. The second advantage is that you already have built up the trust and rapport necessary for a long-term relationship.

- Arrange for a date with someone who subscribes to an online dating service, takes out a personal ad in a newspaper or magazine or registers with a personal dating service.

  These people are available for a relationship. Plus, you can screen potential dates for relevant background information such as age, religion and general interests.

- Ask someone for a date whom you meet while attending singles social events and activities.

  Many of these events are sponsored by religious organizations to service singles of the same faith. In addition, these people may be more motivated to become involved in a long-term relationship.

Five Ways to Attract the Opposite Sex

"It is possible that blondes also prefer gentlemen."
—Mamie Van Doren, American actress, 1933–

Several years ago, I facilitated a workshop called "10 Ways to Attract the Opposite Sex" with Susan Rabin (author of *101 Ways to Flirt;* Plume, 1997). In our workshop, Susan and I asked the participants, "What makes someone attractive?" Surprisingly enough, the answers were more varied than just "good-looking," "great body" and "rich." No question about it, physical appearance and personal success count for a lot, but most people want more substance in a potential mate. Here are the traits and characteristics—other than great looks and money—that most people in the class considered important. To be attractive you can:

1. DISPLAY AN APPROACHABLE AND FRIENDLY DEMEANOR

Take the initiative. Approach those you find attractive, say hello and introduce yourself. Don't forget to smile and shake hands.

2. SHOW YOUR SENSE OF HUMOR

Laugh at other people's jokes. Tell a funny and appropriate story about something that happened to you.

3. BE CONVERSATIONAL AND EASY TO TALK TO

Enjoy the moment and let the other person know you are having fun talking to him or her. Be informal, friendly and animated. Ask questions and talk about upbeat topics. Avoid unpleasant news or downbeat subjects.

4. DISPLAY SELF-CONFIDENCE, SELF-RELIANCE AND A SENSE OF PURPOSE

Be proud of goals you have accomplished and talk about ones you are presently pursuing. Give the other person a sense of what motivates you and why you do what you do. For example, your past or current projects, your school or professional studies, your business endeavors or your sports or physical challenges. At the same time, do not overstate your accomplishments, create an unrealistic image or talk too much about yourself.

5. RESERVE JUDGMENT—ACCEPT OTHERS AS WHO THEY ARE

Allow the other person to be himself or herself. Accept who he or she is without passing judgment—at least not while you are talking.

How to Ask for a Date

A first date can be a short, informal chat over a cup of coffee or a longer, more formal period of time in which you share a meal, see entertainment or go to a party. Whether you meet for thirty minutes or a few hours, a first date is a ritual dance where you and your date discover if you are comfortable, compatible and interested enough in one another to spend more time together. A successful first date would be an agreement to meet for a second, longer date.

OPTION #1: The forty-five-minute first date

Many singles prefer blind dates or first dates with someone they have recently met to be short (less than an hour) and inexpensive. They also chose public places such as a coffee bar or popular park with lots of people around. During that short time, the daters can assess mutual interests and decide if they want to meet again. The advantage of a short date is that both people feel safe and have a limited investment of time and money in the date.

If you like this approach, make your first date a meeting for a drink, coffee, a quick bite to eat or a walk.

"Would you like to meet for a cup of coffee after work?"

"I know a great place to get a quick bite for lunch, if you're interested."

OPTION #2: The formal first date

A first date to an event such as a play or concert or even a visit to a museum can be a good way for two people to get to know each other. For a more formal first date, consider a moderately priced event that you'll both enjoy and that will provide a stepping-off point for more conversation, and hopefully, a second date. Take the risk and say something like.

"I know that you like jazz. There's a concert at my favorite club Friday night. Would you like to go?"

"I have two tickets for a play next Sunday afternoon. I was wondering if you'd like to join me?"

"I've got tickets to a basketball game on Saturday. Would you like to join me?"

ASKING FOR A DATE OVER THE TELEPHONE

If you do not have an opportunity (or nerve) to ask for a date in person, then use the telephone. Always clearly identify yourself or how you know the person. Before you offer an invitation always ask, "Did I catch you at a bad time?" This courtesy offers the person the option to talk later if you have called at an inconvenient time. It is also a good idea to have a few topics of conversation ready if the other person is willing to chat. Say:

"Hello Diane, this is Jack Woods. We met at the chamber of commerce meeting last week. Do you have a minute? Because you said you were a baseball fan, I thought you might like to go to a game with me this weekend. I've got two box seats."

"Hi Sam, this is Gina from down the hall. Say, I know this is short notice, but I just read about a sneak preview playing tomorrow night. I know you're a big film fan. Are you interested in joining me?"

HOW TO SAY "CAN I HAVE A RAIN CHECK?"

If you are interested in going out with a person but the timing is bad, say something like:

"I would have loved to go with you, but I'm busy that night. How about a rain check?"

HOW TO SAY "NO THANK YOU"

If you are asked out on a date but do not want to accept, be honest but polite. You can turn the person down gently by saying:

"No thank you, but it was nice of you to ask."

"I'm not dating right now."

"I'm seeing someone."

How to Handle a Rejection

"You Done Stomped on My Heart and Mashed That Sucker Flat"
—*Country western song written by Mason Williams*

It's inevitable that some people you ask for a date will reject your offer, but that rejection is not the end of the world. Nor should it be the end of your quest to find the right person for you. When you receive a rejection, simply say, "No problem. Maybe another time?"

If your "Maybe another time?" gets a tepid response, consider that as two strikes against you. However, if the other person shows some interest in your offer, then suggest another day or event. As a rule, if someone turns you down three times, accept that he or she is not interested and look for someone else to ask out.

USE POSITIVE SELF-TALK TO HELP GET RID OF FIRST-DATE NERVES

First dates can be nerve-wracking, so use positive self-talk to keep yourself cool and calm. Say to yourself:

"I'm going to have fun on this date."

"Nothing ventured, nothing gained."

"Maybe she (or he) is the love of my life, but I'll never know until we get to know each other."

You now know some of the right and wrong things to do on a first date. But what can you do to turn your first date into a second, third and fourth date?

Twelve Sure Ways to Sabotage Your First Date

Remember the last time you had a bad date? Do you know what you or the other person did to turn your fantasy date into a living nightmare? Chances are, it was one or more of the following ways to sabotage a first date:

1. Pressure the other person to have sex with you.
2. Reveal overly personal information—stories about old boyfriends, health problems or financial woes.
3. Complain about an ex's cheapness, infidelity or poor sexual performance.
4. Come on too strong or sound desperate for a relationship.
5. Talk too loudly or softly.
6. Argue about who is going to pay the bill.
7. Play hard-to-get or try to act mysterious.
8. Chide your date's behavior or criticize his or her views.
9. Wear too much makeup or jewelry.
10. Overindulge in food or alcohol.
11. Talk endlessly about yourself or your interests.
12. Act rudely to people—waiters, cashiers, ushers or other people you meet.

Four Tips for First Dates

"I gave her a look you could have poured on a waffle."
—Ring Lardner, American writer, 1885–1933

When actor Ted Danson talks about his early dates in the book *Bad Dates,* by Carole Markin, he brings up two things. First, he said that because he was six-foot-two in high school he always ended up with the tallest girls. Second, he and his school chums had a cruel tradition called "the Moose Pool." Each guy put in some money and whoever had the "worst" date, won the pool.

One weekend, Ted and his friends all had blinds dates from a local girl's high school. And sure enough, Ted's date was over six feet tall. "She was a lacrosse player. We had nothing in common. Nothing."

During dinner Ted looked around the table at his friends' dates and, because the girl was so tall, he figured he had won the Moose Pool. When the girls were ready to get on the bus to go back to their school, he felt a little guilty that he had not been friendlier, so he said, "Sorry our date didn't turn out so well." The girl smiled and said, "Oh, that's okay because I won the Moose Pool!"

There is no guarantee that your date will be a success. Of course you have first-date jitters! Will it go well? Will you make a major gaff? Will you like your date? Will you fall madly in love and live happily ever after? Or will the date be a big disappointment?

Nothing about a first date is certain. But how your first date turns out and if there is a second date depends largely on how well you get to know each other during the time you spend together. Here are some tips to make your first date successful.

1. DON'T MAKE HAVING SEX THE GOAL OF YOUR FIRST DATE

If having sex is your only goal of a first date, then you are probably not seriously considering this person for an extended relationship. On the other hand, if the two of you hit it off and end up in bed, great—but do not make having sex the criteria for a successful first date.

2. BE YOURSELF AND SHOW YOUR BEST SIDE

Some singles think they have to bend over backward to impress a first date. They may exaggerate their accomplishments, spend lavishly or pretend they are someone they are not. Be on your best behavior, but do not pretend to be someone you are not. Don't lie about your likes or accomplishments to impress your date. If your date does not like who you are, then so be it. On the other hand, when someone enjoys the "real you," your chances of a second date—and maybe even a longer relationship—are good.

3. LEARN ABOUT EACH OTHER

The primary goal of a first date is to find out if you like each other and want to spend more time together. To do that, you both need to share information about yourselves and your background:

- Where you are from

- What brought you to where you are today

- Your vocation

- Where you went to school

- Your religion

- Some family history

Here are some examples of questions and answers that will help you and your date learn more about each other.

Q: "How long have you been living here?"
A: "I've been living in . . . for about . . . years, but originally I'm from. . . ."

Q: "What was it like growing up in . . . ?"
A: "It was great, especially since I was interested in studying . . . in college."

Q: "Where did you go to school?"
A: "Actually I went to a couple schools before I settled down and decide to become a. . . ."

Q: "What kind of work do you do?"
A: "I work in the . . . field. I help people to. . . ."

Q: "How do you spend your time when you're not working?"
A: "When I'm not working I like to. . . ."

How to Handle the Question, "What Do You Do?"

Avoid asking, "What do you do?" to open your conversation. The reason is that many people find this question too abrupt. They are also afraid others will stereotype them or use the answer to determine how much money they make. Instead, ask a few other background questions—where he or she grew up, went to school, what he or she does for fun—before broaching the subject of vocation.

Although I do not recommend asking, "What do you do?" as an ice-breaker, I suggest that you be prepared to answer it directly without making a fuss about it. Also, remember that if you avoid the subject of your vocation for too long, you will appear as if you have something to hide, that you dislike or are ashamed of your job or that you prefer not to talk about what you do for a living.

Q: "What is a favorite thing of yours to do, say on a cold winter afternoon?"
A: "On cold winter weekends I love to cook up a big pot of soup or chili, bake corn bread and share it with a friend."

Q: Do you have any big goals or dreams?"
A: "My career goals are to . . . and my personal goals are to. . . ."

Don't be afraid to ask this most important question—if he or she is available.

Q: "Are you dating anyone special right now?"
A: "I'm dating, but there's no one special right now."

4. GET A SENSE OF YOUR SEXUAL CHEMISTRY

After you chat for a while, you can certainly figure out if there is any sexual chemistry between you. How close do you sit? Are there long glances or warm smiles? What touching has there been between you? Did you hold hands, place a hand or arm on the shoulder or forearm or kiss? If you have a mutual strong physical attraction, do not get pushy. Instead, let nature take its course—on a future date.

Everything has gone great on your first date, and it is nearly over—but not quite. What can you do to end the evening on the right note?

How to End a First Date

"I'll marry you tomorrow, but let's honeymoon tonight."
—Country western song title, writer unknown

Here you are, at the end of your first date. Should you give your date a handshake, a peck on the cheek, a long warm kiss goodnight or an invitation to your place for a nightcap? The answer depends on how you feel about the other person. Did you enjoy yourself enough to want to see the person for a second date? Or was one date is enough? You can reject an offer for a follow-up date without being mean.

HOW TO GIVE A "SOFT" REJECTION FOR A SECOND DATE

Not all first dates lead to a second date. When both people reach that conclusion, you can shake hands, end the date early and that's that. However, if your date suggests that you meet for a second time—but you do not wish to do so, here is how to give a soft rejection.

- Be direct, but not brutally honest.

   Don't say: "You're not my type."
   Do say: "Some people were made for one another, but we're not those people."

- Avoid personal comments.

   Don't say: "There's no chemistry between us."
   Do say: "A romantic relationship between us is not in the cards."

- Don't lie about your current status.

Don't say: "I'm actually involved with someone."
Do say: "I don't want to get into a serious relationship with you."

- Emphasize differences in interests.

  Don't say: "You're boring."
  Do say: "We don't share any common interests."

- Emphasize differences in values.

  Don't say: "You're too opinionated."
  Do say: "We obviously have very different opinions about many things."

- Emphasize differences in goals.

  Don't say: "All you want is sex."
  Do say: "I'm looking for a different kind of relationship than you are."

- Don't make up excuses if you do not want to accept another date.

  Don't say, "I'm awfully busy for the rest of my life."
  Do say: "Thanks for asking, but I'd rather not."

ON YOUR WAY TO A SECOND DATE

When you are on a first date with the right person, you both know it. The two of you have fun, talk, learn about each other, discover common interests, sit close, touch (at least a little) and sense that in time there might be potential for a longer, more intimate relationship.

If you feel good about your first date, do not keep your opinion to yourself. Your date might be feeling the same way but is waiting for a signal from you before revealing his or her feelings. Here is what you can say to let the other person know that you want to see him or her again.

"I really enjoyed myself tonight. How about you?"

"I had fun with you. Can I call you again?"

"You are a terrific person and I really like you. I'd like to see you again."

Surviving and thriving on first dates begins by attracting people who share your interests. You'll make a great first impression when your conversation flows, you laugh and you make the other person feel comfortable. Learn enough about each other before deciding about a second date. After the first date comes the second, third and fourth dates, and soon you are on your way to an intimate relationship—maybe with your soul mate. What could be more exciting than that?

Talking Your Way to a
Long-Term Relationship

"Dear Abby: I am 44 years old and would like to meet a man my age with no bad habits. Signed, Rose.
Dear Rose: So would I."

—from "Dear Abby," syndicated columnist, 1918–

In this chapter, you will learn:
• Turning a friend, coworker or acquaintance into a lover • Seven ways to deepen your relationship • Dos and don'ts when meeting the parents • How to determine your compatibility with your lover • How to break off a relationship or engagement

Love—how do you get it and keep it and what do you do when you lose it? With all the movies, plays, poems, music, art and books on the subject, you might think that finding the love of your life is a cinch, but for many people, the opposite seems true. Perhaps Shakespeare said it best in *A Midsummer Night's Dream* when he wrote, "The course of true love never did run smooth."

But don't give up hope, because there are some ways to improve the odds on finding the right person for a long-term relationship.

Turning a Friend, Coworker or Acquaintance Into a Lover

"Love is not the dying moan of a distant violin—it's the triumphant twain of a bedspring."
                                          —S. J. Perelman, American humorist, 1904–1979

If you are having trouble finding the right person for you, maybe you have overlooked some of your best prospects—your friends, coworkers or business acquaintances. There are risks involved, and most of these people will not fit the bill, but one might—if you are lucky. Before you enter into an office romance, confess your romantic interest to a friend or flirt with a professional acquaintance, consider the following:

- If you are friends, are you willing to risk losing the friendship?

- If you're coworkers, are you willing to risk an uncomfortable situation at work if things don't work out?

- If you have a business relationship, are you willing to change your client-professional status?

All relationships contain a certain amount of risk. Also, remember that some companies frown upon or even prohibit office romances. In addition, some professions consider love relationships with clients a violation of professional ethics. In the end, however, you must decide if the risk is worth the reward.

You have fallen head-over-heels in love! If you are like many singles, you might be thinking about marriage, but don't be too quick to "tie the knot." Spend a lot of time together and deepen your relationship. Then ask yourself again if you and your lover are still game for a long-term relationship.

Seven Ways to Deepen Your Relationship

"You know what I did before I got married? Anything I wanted."
                                          —Henny Youngman, American comedian, 1906–1998

Should You "Date" a Friend? What's Your Opinion?

Is it a good idea to try to turn a friendship into a romantic relationship? Not everyone agrees on this touchy subject. Choose one of the four choices below and then see where you stack up in a recent online survey.

a) No. It's too risky and uncomfortable.
b) Maybe, but I would be afraid that it might spoil the friendship.
c) Yes, because I think it is the best way to start a love relationship.
d) Yes. My spouse was my best friend before we were married.

These are the results of an online poll of about 1,300 people conducted on about.com in July 2001:

• Two percent said no.
• Thirty-one percent said maybe.
• Forty-eight percent said it was the best way.
• Nineteen percent were best friends before they married.

A new love relationship is just about the most exciting thing that can happen to two people. As you spend more time together and get to know each another more intimately, your relationship deepens. When that happens, you will be able to determine if the two of you are suited for a long-term relationship. Here are ways to deepen your relationship:

• Talk about issues, goals and values that are important to both of you.

• Exchange more personal history—especially about your past relationships and your families. (However, you might not want to go into detail about past loves.)

• Discuss what both of you want from a relationship.

• You can say to the other person how you feel about him or her and your relationship. (Do not assume your boyfriend or girlfriend knows how you feel about him or her without you actually saying it aloud.)

- Bring up what you see as differences and see how significant they are to your relationship at present and in the future.

- You can reveal a secret that could affect your relationship. (For example, a medical condition, a financial problem or an unresolved family situation.)

- Talk about your future together and how you would like it to unfold.

Your relationship is going great and you have never felt better about your lover. However, you still need the stamp of approval from some very important people—the parents.

Dos and Don'ts When Meeting the Parents

How you present yourself to your potential in-laws sets the tone for your relationship. Keep in mind that you and your boyfriend's or girlfriend's parents were probably brought up with some different habits, so make an effort to understand their peculiarities or differences. If you want to make a big hit with them, remember these tips:

Do:

- Be friendly and conversational.

- Ask if his or her parents like flowers, specialty foods, wine, etc. and then offer the appropriate gift.

- Flatter the parents by complimenting their home, cooking, yard or other items they are proud of.

- Reveal positive information about yourself.

- Be prepared with several light conversational topics that you know interest the parents. (Ask your boyfriend or girlfriend for suggestions.)

- Expect some quizzing about your background, and be prepared to answer some personal questions.

- Ask your boyfriend or girlfriend about any "taboo topics" to avoid with the parents.

Don't:

- Plan your first meeting on a holiday, at a birthday party, wedding or any other high-pressured formal event.

- Criticize or argue with his or her parents.

- Talk about ex-spouses, relationships or in-laws.

- Talk politics unless you are absolutely certain that you and your potential in-laws are like-minded.

- Show off or try too hard to impress.

- Be overly intimate with your boyfriend or girlfriend while in the parents' home.

- Talk too much about yourself or your work.

- Assume the parents share your sense of humor.

- Expect to be waited on without offering to help.

- Reveal any family secrets.

How to Determine Your Compatibility with Your Lover

"My father told me all about the birds and the bees. The liar—I went steady with a woodpecker till I was twenty-one."

—Bob Hope, American comedian, 1903–

Before you start thinking about marriage, it's wise to consider if you can have a successful relationship. Love may be blind, but you can still listen to that little voice inside your head that tells you how you truly feel. Before you ask, "Will you marry me?" or say "I do," take the following compatibility quiz to see if and your potential spouse are right for each other.

1. Are you in love with each other?
Yes _____ No _____ Not sure _____

2. Do you share a similar sexual appetite?
Yes _____ No _____ Not sure _____

3. Do you feel comfortable talking to each other about personal issues?
Yes _____ No _____ Not sure _____

4. Do you have a strong physical attraction for each other?
Yes _____ No _____ Not sure _____

5. Do you share similar goals for marriage?
Yes _____ No _____ Not sure _____

6. Do you share several common interests?
Yes _____ No _____ Not sure _____

7. Do you share similar religious beliefs?
Yes _____ No _____ Not sure _____

8. Do you share similar political values?
Yes _____ No _____ Not sure _____

9. Have you revealed health issues (past or present illnesses, drug abuse, etc.) that would affect your partner?
Yes _____ No _____ Not sure _____

10. Do you share a desire to have children?
Yes _____ No _____ Not sure _____

11. Do you have similar attitudes about borrowing money and debt?
Yes _____ No _____ Not sure _____

12. Do you enjoy being with each other in your free time?
Yes _____ No _____ Not sure _____

13. Are your spending styles similar?
Yes _____ No _____ Not sure _____

14. Does your "gut" tell you this is the right choice for you?
Yes _____ No _____ Not sure _____

15. Have you spent enough time together—both fun and stressful—to make a reasonable prediction about the success of your relationship?
Yes _____ No _____ Not sure _____

How to score this quiz: Yes = 2 points; no = 0; not sure = 1
Your score: Yes _____ No _____ Not sure _____

Interpreting your score:

25–30 = Take the plunge!
Life is full of surprises, but based on this compatibility quiz, you share enough common attitudes and values about sex, money, religion and politics to give your marriage a good chance of succeeding. There are no guarantees when it comes to love and marriage, but your compatibility quotient is high.

15–25 = Find out more before you commit
You may be in love and physically attracted to one another, but if you and your potential spouse have not compared views about money, child rearing, politics and other values, you could be in for an unpleasant surprise—and may have a life of conflict ahead of you. Take more time to discuss your values, lifestyles and marriage goals. Then take the quiz again and see where you stand.

0–14 = Keep looking for Mr./Ms. Right
You might be smitten with your lover now, but a long-term relationship needs more than dewy-eyed infatuation if it is to succeed. Based on this compatibility quiz, your score suggests that you and your potential spouse share few of the values, goals and attitude that form the basis of a peaceful and long marriage. Don't settle for the wrong person or think that you can change his or her habits. It's better to keep looking for a more compatible person to marry.

But what if you and your lover are not truly compatable? What can you say if you come to the conclusion that continuing the relationship is a bad idea?

How to Break Off a Relationship or Engagement

"Love is like war. Easy to begin but very hard to stop."
—H. L. Mencken, American editor and critic, 1880–1956

If anyone knows about breaking off relationships, it's career husband-hunter, Zsa Zsa Gabor. Married nine times, she once hosted a TV show devoted to marriage problems. Moments after the first guest came on stage, she confessed to Zsa Zsa, "I'm breaking my engagement to a very wealthy man who has already given me a sable coat, diamonds, a stove and a Rolls-Royce. Miss Gabor, what should I do?"

Zsa Zsa answered, "Give back the stove."

For better or worse, not all love relationships or engagements result in marriages. What do you do and say to break off a relationship? How can you soften the blow and cause the other person the least amount of pain? Is it better to tell your boyfriend or girlfriend face-to-face, over the telephone or in a letter? Here are three tips to follow when you quit a long-term or serious relationship.

TIP #1: Be direct and calm and practice what you want to say

If you shout or blame the other person for the breakup (even if he or she deserves it), you will just make both of you feel worse. You might owe the other person an explanation for your decision, but make it brief and frame it in terms of what's best for both of you.

To break off a relationship you might say:

"I've thought a lot about this. I've decided that it's best for both of us if we break off our relationship."

"I've decided that I want to be single again. It's taken me a while to realize that we want very different things from a relationship."

To break an engagement to be married, you can say:

"Something has happened that has made me have second thoughts about getting married."

"I think it would be a mistake if we got married."

"I'm sorry, I've changed my mind, but I made a mistake agreeing (or asking) to marry you."

"I want to call off our engagement."

TIP #2: Choose an uneventful time to break the news

Avoid breaking up at a sentimental time such as a holiday or birthday, during an illness or during a stressful time at work. No time will seem like a good time to break the news. The best you can do is to choose a time when there is no emergency. You can say:

> "I know that this is not a good time for you and that you are going to get upset, but I've decided I want out of our relationship (engagement)."

TIP #3: Break the news at his or her place

Opinions vary on where the best place is to break up with someone. Some people feel that meeting in a public place, face-to-face, is best and most respectful. Others believe the most tactful way to deliver the bad news is in private. Some people choose the telephone or a letter.

Breaking up in a public or neutral place—a café or park bench, for example—might be wise if you fear the other person may have a physical or emotional outburst or you do not want to be alone with him or her when you break the news. However, being in public by no means guarantees a quiet response, so be prepared for an emotional scene.

Choosing to break the news in the other person's home, on the other hand, allows you to leave after you have said your piece and lets him or her react in private. If your ex bursts into tears, screams and shouts or slams the bedroom door, then he or she can do so without embarrassment.

Here are some other alternatives: You can break up with the other person over the telephone or, if you are in a long-distance relationship, in a letter. These methods also allow you to break the news in private

What to Tell Yourself to Survive a Breakup

Whether you are the one breaking up or the one who has been dumped, ending a relationship leaves both people with bruised egos and hurt feelings. You might know that breaking up was for the best, but you can still feel upset, uncertain and lonely. Here is what you can say to yourself to maintain you sense of self-respect and get yourself psyched into being single again.

Tell yourself, "You are a survivor."
Acting and thinking like a "survivor" will help you gain the confidence you need to get through some of the difficult times that lie ahead. You can say something like:

"I am a survivor, and I'll get through this."

"I'll find someone who is right for me."

"I know this is the best thing for both of us."

"It's better to do this now than later."

"I may be alone for a while, but that's better than being in an unhappy relationship."

without putting you or your (now) ex in an embarrassing or compromising situation.

Cowardly Ways to Break Up

- Saying that you're going back with an ex-spouse or former girl-friend or boyfriend

- Saying that you've found someone else you like better

- Suddenly not calling or becoming unavailable

- Using the silent treatment, picking fights, being mean, withholding affection, cheating or flirting until the other person gets fed up and breaks it off

- Repeatedly breaking up and getting back together until the other person gets fed up and finally calls it quits for good

- E-mailing or faxing a letter saying you are breaking up

"Tis better to have loved and lost than never to have loved at all."
—Alfred, Lord Tennyson, British poet, 1809–1892

When it comes to relationships, there are no guarantees, no matter how much you are in love or how well suited you believe you are for one another. However, the more compatible you are with your lover (and his or her parents), the better your chances are for a successful relationship. Friendships—if the chemistry is there for both people—can lead to a deep and long-lasting romance.

CHAPTER NINETEEN

Messages That Make Your Marriage Work

"EGGHEAD WEDS HOURGLASS"

> *—1956* Variety *headline on the marriage of playwright Henry Miller*
>
> *to actress Marilyn Monroe*

In this chapter, you will learn:
• **Four communication styles that newlyweds need to know** • **How to discuss issues that affect your marriage** • **Nine ground rules for fighting fair** • **Eight ways to show you appreciate your spouse**

Four Communication Styles That Newlyweds Need to Know

> *"I was incredible in bed last night. I never once had to sit up and consult the manual."*
>
> *—Woody Allen, American comedian, 1935–*

Two married men were discussing how they talked with their wives and made family decisions. One fellow said, "First of all, I wear the pants in my family. I make all the decisions, and what I say goes. What about you?"

"Well," his friend said, "my wife and I talked it over on our honeymoon and we agreed to a perfect plan. I decide all the major matters and she decides the minor ones."

"So how has it worked out?" the friend asked.

"So far," he said, "no major matters have come up."

Do you and your spouse have different styles of communicating?

How can newlyweds successfully integrate their communication styles into their new life? The first step is to identify how you and your spouse communicate. Here are the four common communication styles and some strategies to help you get along better.

STRAIGHTFORWARD STYLE

Spouses who have a straightforward speaking style are energetic, motivated and competitive. Many display these speaking characteristics:

Positive:

- Get to the point quickly

- Are talkative about topics that interest them

- Have strong opinions and see conversations as contests

Negative:

- Are poor listeners who frequently interrupt

- Make blunt comments and impulsive decisions

- Become domineering and argumentative

Communication Strategies

If your spouse has a straightforward communication style, use these strategies:

- Begin a conversation by discussing topics of interest to him or her.

- Avoid reacting to provocative statements or accusations.

- Listen for and acknowledge areas of agreement.

- Follow up with topics you wish to discuss. Do not passively wait for your spouse to ask you about what you want to talk about.

- Make your main point first. Then follow it with one or two supporting details—and not the other way around.

- If your spouse disagrees, do not back off right away or get defensive. He or she might be testing you or trying to get you into a debate. Instead, offer a few details to support your views. If he or she attempts to argue, say, "I don't want to get into a debate or argument. I'm just telling you how I see it from my point of view."

SOCIABLE STYLE

Spouses who have a sociable speaking style are energetic, like to talk things over and are eager to please. Many display these speaking characteristics:

Positive:

- Are talkative about a variety of topics

- Appear interested in their spouse's views and feelings

- Seek light and congenial conversation

Negative:

- Ramble, chatter, finish sentences or interrupt

- Make impulsive decisions

- Are overeager for praise and attention

Communication Strategies

If your spouse has a sociable communication style, use these strategies:

- Discuss topics of mutual interest to both of you.

- Do not let your spouse dominate the conversation.

- Interject your comments and questions.

- Acknowledge and praise areas of agreement.

- Actively bring up topics you wish to discuss if your spouse fails to ask you about them.

- Offer your main point first, followed by other details.

- If your spouse interrupts, say, "Please, let me finish what I have to say."

RESERVED STYLE

Spouses who have a reserved speaking style are quiet, sensitive to others, consider decisions carefully and avoid confrontation. Many display these speaking characteristics:

Positive:

- Listens attentively for the feelings behind the words

- Are interested in their spouse's views and feelings

- Seeks congenial conversation and ways to help others solve problems

Negative:

- Appears withdrawn or uncommunicative

- Is passive or unassertive with dominant speakers

- Avoids sharing preferences or making decisions if challenged

Communication Strategies

If your spouse has a reserved communication style, use these strategies:

- Avoid dominating the conversation or interrupting.

- Gently interject your comments and questions.

- Gently probe for topics that interest him or her *before* you talk about what interests you.

- Acknowledge areas of agreement.

- Avoid a loud voice or aggressive body language.

- Make your main point and follow it with more details.

- Ask your spouse for his or her opinion by saying, "Please, tell me what you think about. . . ."

RATIONAL STYLE

Spouses who have a rational speaking style are logical, quiet and serious. Many display these speaking characteristics:
Positive:

- Are knowledgeable about complicated topics

- Speak in detail from start to finish

- Seek to be accurate and correct in what they say

Negative:

- Think emotions are less important than logic when making decisions

- Control or dominate others

- Are inflexible about what they think is right

Communication Strategies

If your spouse has a rational communication style, use these strategies:

- Offer your main point followed by factual details that support your views.

- Balance talking and listening by interjecting your comments and questions.

- Be assertive but avoid confrontation.

- Avoid criticism based on emotion or instinct.

- Acknowledge and praise areas of agreement.

- Actively bring up topics you wish to discuss if your spouse fails to ask you about them.

- If your spouse negates your views because they are illogical, say "You might be right about that, but good decisions are not based solely on logic."

Keep in mind that you and your spouse use a combination of communication styles. When you hear your spouse say something that could easily be misconstrued, ask him or her for clarification. You can ask something like:

"You seem to be saying. . . . Am I right?"

"I'm not sure I understand you correctly. Can you give me an example of what you mean?"

"You didn't come right out and say so, but I get the impression that . . . Is that correct?"

Now you know about the building blocks of a solid marriage and can communicate smoothly. That's great, because you will need every communication skill you can muster when you need to talk with your spouse about a sensitive subject.

How to Discuss Issues That Affect Your Marriage

"You don't marry one person; you marry three—the person you think they are, the person they are, and the person they are going to become as the result of being married to you."

—Richard Needham, Canadian columnist, 1912–1996

Actor Robert Mitchum (1917–1997) was once asked what he believed was the secret of his more than fifty years of marriage to his wife, Dorothy, especially when so many other Hollywood couples broke up. "Mutual forbearance," he replied. "We have each continued to believe that the other will do better tomorrow."

Optimism is certainly an essential ingredient to a long and successful relationship, but so is talking about the issues that determine the direction of your marriage. The sooner you and your spouse discuss, clarify and reach agreements on these issues, the fewer arguments you will have about them later. Here are some questions you can ask to bring up some sensitive topics.

TALKING ABOUT CHILDREN

"When—if ever—should we have kids?"

"What's your view on disciplining kids?"

"What can we do to encourage them?"

"How much responsibility should we give them?"

"How should we spend time with them?"

TALKING ABOUT HEALTH

"What did the doctor tell you?"

"How are you feeling right now?"

"How does your problem with . . . affect you?"

"What can you tell me about your medical problem?"

TALKING ABOUT MONEY

"How much money do we need to live on each month?"

"Who is going to pay the bills?"

"How do feel about buying things on credit?"

"How much can we afford to spend on a home?"

"How much money should we save each month?"

"Do you think we should buy a used or new car?"

TALKING ABOUT POLITICS

"What are your opinions of the candidates running in this year's election?"

"Where do you stand on the issues of . . . ?"

TALKING ABOUT PAST RELATIONSHIPS

"What was your previous marriage like?"

"How did your and your ex deal with problems?"

"How do we deal with our ex-spouses at birthday parties, weddings and holiday get-togethers?"

TALKING ABOUT DEATH

"How do we explain Grandma's death to the kids?"

"What should we include in our will?"

"Whom do you think should be the executor for our will?"

"What kind of funeral service do you want?"

"Do you want a living will?"

When you discuss sensitive topics, you have an opportunity to compare views and exchange ideas. If you open a "can of worms" that leads to intense discussions, avoid losing your temper or arguing. Instead, listen for areas of agreement and keep an open mind for ways to find common ground and reach compromises.

Talking about what you do and how you feel—your day at work, the kids, or even sensitive subjects is the primary way you communicate your thoughts and feelings to your spouse. But how do you handle situations in which you and your spouse don't see eye-to-eye?

Nine Ground Rules for Fighting Fair

"Marriage is for a little while. It's alimony that is forever."
—Quentin Crisp, British author and wit, 1908–1999

Do you have big fights over the same old problems? Have you tried talking things out and still ended up in shouting matches that leave you in tears or facing a chilly silence? Have you had it up to here with excuses or empty promises? Do you or your spouse threaten to end your marriage? If these situations describe your marriage, then you may be headed for a breakup.

However, do not throw in the towel and scrap your marriage just yet. You may be able to save your relationship, but you must agree to talk and attempt to resolve your differences. Here is how you can present this idea to your spouse. Say:

"I'm afraid that our marriage can't survive if it keeps going this way. I think our marriage is worth saving. Do you? If you agree with me, let's sit down, talk like adults and try to work out some of our problems. Are you willing to talk about it?"

If your spouse agrees, then ask him or her to agree to these ground rules:

GROUND RULE #1: No shouting

Speaking calmly encourages you and your spouse to listen to each other. In addition, when you speak in a calm tone you are less likely to say things that incite your partner or make accusations that you might later regret. Before you begin your discussion, ask:

"Can we agree to talk without shouting at each other?"

If your voice becomes emotional and rises in volume and pitch, stop speaking for a moment. Imagine lowering the volume of your voice with a knob on your stereo or button on your TV remote control. You can even say:

"I'm getting upset. I need a moment to calm down."

If your partner breaks this rule, you can say:

"We agreed to speak to each other without shouting."

GROUND RULE #2: No name-calling

Use your spouse's name when you address him or her. Avoid calling him or her names, such as "louse," "cheap," "cheat," "stupid," "irresponsible," "thoughtless," "selfish" and so on—even though the terms may be apt. Ask:

"Can we agree to not call each other names?"

If, however, you slip and call your spouse a name, quickly apologize by saying:

"Sorry, I promised not to call you any names."

If your partner breaks this rule, you can say:

"We agreed that we would not call each other names."

GROUND RULE #3: Discuss one problem at a time

If you try to talk about too many problems at once, the task will be overwhelming and most likely disintegrate into a shouting match. Instead, talk about one issue at a time. Discuss it and, if possible, settle on a compromise. Ask:

"We have a lot of disagreements, but we can't solve all our problems at once. Can we agree to start by talking about just one of our problems? You can choose first, if you want."

If your partner declines, then you can say:

"I'd like to resolve our problem with. . . ."

If your partner breaks this rule, you can say:

"We agreed to talk about one issue at a time."

GROUND RULE #4: No interrupting

Listen without interruption, especially if your spouse accuses you of something, even if in your heart you know he or she is wrong or is making an unfair accusation. Remaining quiet and poised shows you are listening and that you take your spouse's words seriously. Ask:

"Can we agree to let each other finish speaking without interrupting?"

If you interrupt your spouse, say:

"I'm sorry, I interrupted you. Go on."

If your partner breaks this rule, you can say:

"We agreed that we wouldn't interrupt each other."

GROUND RULE #5: No stomping out of the room

Listening to harsh criticism can make anyone want to storm out of the room in a huff, especially when emotions are running high. Ask:

"Can we agree to hear each other out without stomping out of the room?"

If you feel like bolting from the room, hang tough and listen for the real issues. After your spouse has finished speaking, if you still feel the need to cool off or figure out your response, ask for a short break. You can say:

> "Now that you're finished, I need a few minutes alone to think about what you've said."

Keeping a neutral tone can soften criticism and encourage your spouse to listen. However, if your partner gets up to leave in a fit of anger, you can say:

> "We agreed to not leave the room when the other person speaks. Please let me finish. Then let's take a break."

GROUND RULE #6: No bringing up past arguments

You might be tempted to bring up past arguments. However, flinging old accusations back and forth will only make both of you angrier. Then it will be nearly impossible to find any common points that you can agree on. Ask:

> "Can we agree to keep our past arguments out of this and stick to what we've agreed to talk about?"

If your partner breaks this rule, you can say:

> "We agreed that we wouldn't bring up old arguments."

GROUND RULE #7: No blaming

Spouses routinely blame each other for their marriage problems. You probably both have legitimate complaints or issues that need to be addressed. Ask:

> "Can we agree not to blame each other for what's gone wrong and focus on how we can improve our marriage?"

If your partner breaks this rule, you can say:

"We agreed not to blame each other. Let's just stick to what we agreed to talk about."

GROUND RULE #8: Stick to the facts

If your marriage is in trouble, half-truths or white lies will only create more distrust and anger. It is better to be truthful and deal with it. Ask:

"Can we agree to be truthful with one another?"

If you have lied to your spouse in the past, do not continue to avoid the truth. Simply say:

"I haven't been truthful with you."

If your partner breaks this rule, you can say:

"We agreed that we would stick to the facts."

GROUND RULE #9: If necessary, seek professional counseling

If you are unable to reach even a minimal agreement after trying to talk out a problem, you might need to seek the assistance of a professional counselor. Ask:

"Can we agree that if we aren't able to work out our problems by ourselves, we'll see a marriage counselor together?"

If your partner decides not to cooperate, you can say:

"We agreed that if we couldn't resolve our problems, we would see a marriage counselor. Our marriage is on the line. I'm making an appointment to see a marriage counselor. Will you come with me?"

Setting ground rules for discussing difficult issues affecting your marriage can make a big difference to you and your spouse. Marriage is never easy, and of course, it takes effort. One way to keep your marriage healthy is to show your spouse how much you care.

Eight Ways to Show You Appreciate Your Spouse

"Baby, you're the greatest!"
—*Ralph Kramden (played by Jackie Gleason, 1916–1987)*

All husbands and wives have minor misunderstandings, but most are quickly resolved. However, an equally common problem that causes conflict is the failure to show appreciation for the little things your spouse does for you. That mistake, if left uncorrected, can hurt even a solid marriage. In some instances, not showing appreciation is an underlying cause of sniping, nagging or major arguments over minor things—like whether to buy crunchy or smooth peanut butter.

Everyone wants to feel appreciated—especially your spouse, so why not give out what you want in return. Here are a few examples of what you can say and do to show your spouse how much you appreciate all the things—both big and little—that he or she does for you.

1. Finally do something that your spouse has asked you to do a hundred times. This could be anything from (men) helping with the dishes and picking up your clothes to (women) putting the top back on the toothpaste tube or mowing the lawn.

   Say, "Guess what, I'm going to . . . just for you."

2. Take your spouse out for a special night on the town. It does not need to be expensive or extravagant. A nice dinner and a movie (of your spouse's choice) may do the trick.

   Say, "Let's do something we enjoy but haven't done in a long time."

3. Bring your spouse home a special treat to eat. This could be chocolates, cookies or jellybeans.

   Say, "Sweets for the sweet."

4. Most women love a surprise gift of cut flowers. Of course, be prepared for a few suspicious looks and the question, "Okay, what's up with the flowers?"

   Say, "I just wanted to show you know how much I love and appreciate you."

5. Plan a special event for your spouse other than his or her birthday or your anniversary. Send the kids to a baby-sitter and plan a romantic evening at home or a fantastic night on the town.

   Say, "Let's do something special just for us."

6. Take your spouse to lunch. You entertain your clients to show them you appreciate their business, so why not do the same thing for your husband or wife? Small gestures send the message:

   "I appreciate all the things you do for me."

7. Surprise your spouse with a romantic card.

   Say, "Just a note to tell you that I love you every day—and not just on Valentine's Day."

8. Sharing the credit is as important as sharing the reward of your accomplishments. Give your spouse credit for his or her efforts on your behalf.

   Say, "Thanks for all your help. I couldn't have done it without you."

You and your spouse want to feel appreciated, and not just on special occasions, but every day. When spouses tell and show how much they appreciate each other, their relationship reaps the rewards.

"The critical period in matrimony is breakfast-time."
                    —A. P. Herbert, British politician and writer, 1890–1971

Happy marriages just don't happen—they are built on intimacy, trust and good communication. Talk with your spouse about the issues that affect your marriage—such as children, work, money and your future—and learn how to compromise and resolve your differences. Remember, never underestimate the power of praise, affection and appreciation.

CHAPTER TWENTY

Talking to Kids, Parents
and Relatives

"A family is a unit composed not only of children, but of men, women, an occasional animal and the common cold."

—Ogden Nash, American writer, 1902–1971

In this chapter, you will learn:
• **How to get great results with kids** • **Three strategies for handling pushy parents and in-laws** • **Eight things you can say to mend a family rift** • **Two difficult questions to discuss with an aging parent** • **Things you should never say at family get-togethers**

A normally patient father finally lost his temper at the Thanksgiving dinner table while trying to settle a squabble between several family members. "Everyone always has to get his way around here," he bellowed. "What about me? When do I get my way, for once?" The little girl seated next to her father tugged on his sleeve and whispered, "It's really quite easy," she said, "just cry a little."

How to Get Great Results with Kids

"Be nice to your children. After all, they are going to choose your nursing home."

—Steven Wright, American comedian, 1955–

Art Linkletter, longtime host of the 1950s TV show *Kids Say the Darndest Things,* knew the secret to getting the best comments from the kids whom he interviewed. After he asked for their opinions, he listened to what they said. In addition, he made them laugh and feel important. You, too, can get great results with your children when you:

1. Smile and show genuine interest in what they do and say. Ask:

   "What are you working on (building, drawing, playing, making, etc.)?"

2. Ask for their ideas, thoughts, opinions and feelings about events, issues or popular culture that interests them. Kids will tell your what they think and feel—if you ask them. Ask:

   "What do you think of the new Harry Potter book (movie, video game, etc.)? Do you like (dislike) it?"

   "What is it that you like so much about . . . ?"

   "What do you enjoy doing most after you're finished with school and homework?"

3. Frequently praise their good qualities. Say:

   "You're really good at. . . ."

   "You've a real talent for. . . ."

4. Kids—like adults—are more likely to do what you ask when you show them basic respect and kindness. Say:

   "Please. . . ." and "Thank you for. . . ."

   "I really appreciate it when you help me. Thanks."

5. Communicate reasonable rules and enforce them.

Although children sometimes protest about rules, they usually feel more secure when their parents set and enforce reasonable restrictions. Say:

"You know the rules. Please follow them."

"We agreed that you would . . . only after you. . . ."

"You might not agree with me, but I'm your parent and what I say goes."

6. Admit and apologize when (not if) you make a mistake.

Kids know that everyone—even their parents—make mistakes. Take advantage of this by showing you know how to accept responsibility and learn from your mistakes, especially when it involves your kids. They will respect you for it and learn by your example. Say:

"I shouldn't have accused you of. . . . I made a mistake, and I apologize."

"Sorry about that. I messed up."

"It was my fault that. . . ."

7. Encourage kids, whenever possible, to reach their own conclusions and decisions by asking questions and discussing issues. Ask questions like:

"So how do you plan on handling the situation?"

"If you were a teacher, what would you tell a student who . . . ?"

"The choice is yours as long as I approve. What are the pros and cons?"

SHOWING KIDS RESPECT BUILDS THEIR SELF-ESTEEM

The words you use when you speak to your child can either build or diminish his or her self-esteem. At the same time, respect is a two-way street. Showing respect for your child's opinions—even if they are different than yours—encourages him or her to respect and consider your views. Avoid creating conflict or making comments that undermine your child's self-esteem and confidence.

Don't say: "You shouldn't feel that way."
Do say: "I remember feeling that way once, too."

Don't say: "That's ridiculous!"
Do say: "Why do you feel that way?"

Don't say: "That's the dumbest thing I've ever heard."
Do say: "That's a creative (different, unusual, new, etc.) way of looking at it."

Don't say: "You should find better friends."
Do say: "Don't let your friends make your decisions."

Don't say: "How could you be so stupid?"
Do say: "Everyone makes mistakes. Learn from them and do it better the next time."

Don't say: "What makes you think that you could ever succeed at . . . ?"
Do say: "Some people you'd never expect to be good at . . . end up being great. . . ."

Don't say: "You wouldn't be any good at. . . ."
Do say: "Give it a try and see how you like it. Then decide if you want to continue."

Don't say: "You don't know what you're talking about."
Do say: "Can you back up your statement with facts, or are you only expressing your opinion?"

Don't say: "Don't do as I do, do as I say."
Do say: "I try to set a good example for you, but I make my share of mistakes, too.

Don't say: "You're a quitter."
Do say: "Some things take a bit of extra effort if you are to succeed. Keep it at, and you'll see that you can do it."

Your words have a great impact on your children. When you talk to them not only as your kids, but as people, too, you will build mutual respect and trust for a lifetime.

Three Strategies for Handling Pushy Parents and In-Laws

*"I can't help detesting my relations. I suppose it comes from the fact that
none of us can stand other people having the same faults as ourselves."*
                      —Oscar Wilde, Irish-born British playwright, 1845–1900

On his visit to the United States, French soldier Marshal Foch (1851–
1929) wanted to see the Grand Canyon. As he gazed over the vast ex-
panse, he turned to the fellow next to him and remarked, "What a mar-
velous place to drop one's mother-in-law."

Parents and other relatives—mother-in-laws in particular—may be
the butt of many jokes, but it's no laughing matter when they constantly
pressure and cajole you and your spouse into doing things their way. The
trouble is, if you disagree with them, they will call you ungrateful, sulk
or, if things do not work out how you planned, say, "I told you so!"

On the other hand, if you cave in to your parents' every suggestion,
they will try to control every aspect of your life—from where you live to
how you raise your kids to what you eat. So how can you keep domineering parents or in-laws from smothering you?

Retaining your independence without getting into fights—or God forbid, being disinherited—takes tact, resolve and knowing when to give in
to get your way. The following three strategies will help you keep domineering parents and in-laws in check.

STRATEGY #1: Choose your battles

If you haven't figured it out already, your parents' and in-laws' encroach-
ment into your married life will never end, so don't turn their every suggestion into a fight. Yes, you might win a few of the battles, but in the
end, you will lose the war. (Do not think for a moment that your marriage will not suffer if you are on bad terms with your parents or in-
laws.) The best action is to pluck a few of your parents' and in-laws'
good ideas, give them the credit they crave and then figure out the rest
for yourselves.

STRATEGY #2: Don't argue—listen

Most parents and in-laws have a strong desire to play roles as experienced
advisers. It makes them feel important when they help you get what you

want (or what they think you should want). However, you will only frustrate, irritate and alienate them if your first impulse to their well-meaning advice is to snap, "Mind your own business!"

Instead, pause for a moment of silence after you hear the suggestion and take a deep breath. Look him or her in the eye and say:

"I'm listening. Go on."

"Interesting idea. How would you go about doing it?"

"What else would you do to handle the situation?"

"What would be the next step?"

"How would that move affect our plans to . . . ?"

If you really want to score some big points with your parent or in-law, ask:

"Can I ask you for some advice?"

Now watch a smile of satisfaction spread over your parent's or in-law's face as he or she elaborates. By listening, you can also objectively decide whether the advice is useful. After all, most parents and in-laws have some good ideas or can help you solve problems, and it would be self-defeating to ignore them simply out of spite or closed-mindedness. The more you let your parents or in-laws play the roles of trusted advisers, the happier they will be. Just do not let them overdo it.

STRATEGY #3: Make your own decisions

Handling domineering parents and in-laws requires that you and your spouse make your own decisions and live with the consequences. And do not be shy about expressing what you think, but do it in a nice way. You can tell them that you appreciate their input and help by saying something like:

"Thanks for sharing your thoughts with us. We'll let you know what we decide to do."

"Talking to you really helps. Thanks. We haven't made a final decision yet, but we're getting closer."

"We like your ideas about . . . but we are not sure that . . . fits in to our overall plan. We still need to think more about what we've discussed."

Be prepared for more pressure, cajoling and downright disapproval if you postpone a decision, do not follow all their advice or make a decision with which they disagree. Here is what you can say:

"We appreciate all that you do for us and your advice, too. But in the end, we have to do what we think is best for us."

Five Things You Can Say to Mend a Family Rift

"Better a thousand enemies outside the house than one inside."
—*Arabic proverb*

Family squabbles, feuds and frosty relations hurt every member of the family. In addition, the longer the family conflicts last, the more pain they cause. It takes humility to admit a mistake and then to apologize for saying or doing something that caused a family rift. Likewise, accepting an apology shows you can forgive and move on. Sometimes, all it takes is for one person to take the first step. You can be the one to bring harmony and happiness back into your family. Here is what you can say:

"I don't think our disagreement is worth hurting our family, do you?"

"I'm letting it go. I hope you can, too."

"I admit I was wrong. I apologize."

"Let's just agree to disagree and leave it."

"I hope we can put the past behind us."

DIFFICULT QUESTIONS TO DISCUSS WITH AN AGING PARENT

"Don't worry about senility. When it hits you, you won't know it."
—Bill Cosby, American comedian, 1937–

Cartoonist Al Hirschfeld (1903–) has captured the most famous faces in show business—from Charlie Chaplin to Whoopi Goldberg—for more than 70 years. Today, the near centenarian still surrounds himself with his pencils, India ink, erasers and brushes. "This is where I enjoy myself," he says. When interviewed for a documentary about his career he said, "I'm not interested in what comes next or what was before. I'm interested in the here and now."

Making decisions with your aging parent is very much dealing with the "here and now." According to eldercare experts, joint decision-making, whenever possible, is the best way to maintain a harmonious day-to-day relationship between an adult child and his or her aging parent.

Based on his or her ability and desire to do so, your aging parent can make the majority of the decisions about daily living issues. However, eldercare experts strongly suggest bringing up and discussing these two critical questions with your aging parent *before* they require immediate decisions.

QUESTION #1: Should your aging parent live at home or in an assisted-living facility?

Discussing the pros and cons of these living options will help you and your parent reach the right decision. Here is what you can say:

"The time is approaching when you'll need help with preparing meals, cleaning and so on. You don't need to make any decisions now, but you'll need to think about what would be best for you and me. You can continue to live here with help coming in, or you could live in a retirement community where the services are provided. Which do you think you might prefer?"

If you feel that assisted living offers the best alternative for your parent and you, first bring up pros and cons of living at home. You can say:

"I think the biggest benefit of remaining at home is that you are in familiar surroundings."

"But there are also some cons. Will you remember to take all your medications? Moreover, what will you do if you have a medical problem, or what if—God forbid—you were to slip and fall? Do you understand why I worry about you living here alone?"

Then explain, "I think there are some real advantages to assisted living."

"They provide all the housekeeping, meals, medical, recreation, transportation and security. You don't need to worry about a thing, and neither will I. Plus, you will have plenty of people around to keep you company."

Finding the right assisted-living community for your parent and your pocketbook

Assisted-living residences vary widely in services and rates. Never ask your parent to agree to live in a residence without first:

- Getting two or three recommendations

- Visiting several residences alone to eliminate any poor choice

- Taking your parent to a few good facilities

- Talking to some of the residents

- Comparing facilities, their costs and services

QUESTION #2: Should you limit or discontinue your aging parent's driving?

For many aging adults, driving and independence are equated with self-esteem. Of course, you want your parent to continue to be independent as long as possible. However, if he or she cannot drive safely, then you and your parent need to make some changes.

How do you know when that time has come for your parent to limit or discontinue his or her driving? First, take a drive with your parent and silently evaluate his or her skills. Then ask your parent the following questions to see if the time is right to talk about changing his or her driving practices:

1. Have you had two or more fender benders within the last month or so? Yes _____ No _____

2. Have you had two or more moving violations within the last month or so? Yes _____ No _____

3. Have you had more than two close calls in the last month? Yes _____ No _____

4. Have you had a serious accident within the last several months? Yes _____ No _____

5. Do you have trouble using your hands to steer or your feet to push the pedals? Yes _____ No _____

6. Do you get flustered when you merge into traffic, change lanes or turn left at a stop light? Yes _____ No _____

7. Do you drive 15 mph slower than the posted speed limit? Yes _____ No _____

8. Do you see traffic signs less well at night? Yes _____ No _____

9. Do passengers appear nervous when they drive with you? Yes _____ No _____

10. Do other drivers honk at you, or do pedestrians shout at you? Yes _____ No _____

11. Do you have difficulty turning your head to see the lanes on either side of your car? Yes _____ No _____

12. Do you get anxious driving in heavy traffic? Yes _____ No _____

13. Do you slow down when you come to an intersection with a green light? Yes _____ No _____

14. Do you sometimes forget how to get to familiar places?
    Yes _____ No _____

15. Have other family members expressed their concern to you about your driving? Yes _____ No _____

How to score: Yes = 1; no = 0 Total score: _____
What the scores mean:

If your parent's score is 0–3 = Okay for now

This score suggests that your parent is a capable and a safe driver—for now—but still talk to him or her about driving safety. Take a closer look at the "yes" answers to make any necessary changes you think will make your parent a safer driver. (Some parents may bend the truth a little.) Keep a steady watch for any needed adjustments to his or her driving practices.

If your parent's score is 4–7 = Curtail driving

This score suggests that your parent is having some difficulty driving safely in certain situations and conditions. This is definitely the time to talk to him or her about driving safety. Gently and respectfully, suggest the following changes in his or her driving patterns. Say:

> "Dad (Mom), I want to talk to you about your driving. You're a good driver, but I think it's time for you to stop driving at night, during rush hour, on the freeway or over long distances."

Keep a steady watch for any additional adjustments to his or her driving practices.

If your parent's score is 9–15 = Stop driving

This score indicates that it is time for your parent to give up driving. Most seniors do not want to give up their car keys, but if your parent continues to operate an automobile, he or she is posing a risk to others as well as him- or herself. You can bring up the topic gently and tactfully by saying:

"Mom (Dad), this last fender-bender (ticket, close call, etc.) is the third one this month. I think it's time to call it quits and hang up your car keys before you have a more serious accident and you or someone else gets hurt."

If your parent vehemently resists or denies he or she has a driving problem, ask your family physician to speak with him or her. Aging parents often will take their doctor's advice. If not, then suggest a visit to the motor vehicle office for a driver's test and examination to settle the issue.

You can also suggest other transportation alternatives such as walking, car pools, public transportation, friends, relatives, bicycles or special senior citizen services. Finally you can say:

"I don't want to be the one who has to make the decision that you cannot drive anymore. I think you can make the decision for yourself. It shows that you still have good judgment and know the right and safe thing to do."

DOS AND DON'TS FOR DEALING WITH AGING PARENTS

Communicating with an aging parent frequently tests your persuasive skills and patience. Keep in mind the following dos and don'ts when talking to your aging parent.

Do:

- Spend time with your parents so you can evaluate their situation

- Talk with a family friend, relative or physician to discuss your parents' health, home life and driving

- Bring up your concerns with your aging parents before they become emergencies

- Remain patient and allow extra time for your parents to process what they hear, formulate answers or questions and make decisions

- Stay calm and keep the tone of your voice friendly—never condescending

- Explain that everyone in your family needs to make some adjustments as the parents' situation changes

Don't:

- React with an angry response when they push your "old buttons"

- Lecture or talk down to your aging parent

- Expect them to remember everything you say

- Use disrespectful or harsh language

- Threaten use of excessive pressure to force your parent to do things against his or her will

- Expect your aging parents to change their habits without frequent reminders

Things You Should *Never* Say at Family Birthday Parties, Dinners, Wedding or Funerals

"You see this watch? This is an absolutely fantastic, very fine elegant gold watch which speaks of breeding and was sold to me by my grandfather on his deathbed."

—Woody Allen, American comedian, 1935–

At a large wedding reception, the father of the bride was shaking hands and thanking several of the guests and relatives for attending, when he found himself saying so long to the groom's mother for a second time. "But you've already said good night to me," she snorted.

"Ah yes, so I have," he replied, "but it is always such a pleasure to say good-bye to you."

Family gatherings—birthday parties, holiday dinners, weddings and funerals—offer special opportunities to put your foot in your mouth. Here are several examples of what *not* to say in those situations:

FAUX PAS AT BIRTHDAY PARTIES

"You look great. Have you had cosmetic surgery?"

"Now that you're getting on in years, do you find that you're having trouble with . . . ?"

"Have you put on weight?"

"How old are you—really?"

FAUX PAS AT FAMILY DINNERS

"Dear, you have many talents, but cooking, I'm afraid is not one of them."

"Sorry, we need to leave early. We want to visit some friends."

"It must have been something I ate."

"I thought you knew that I was allergic to. . . ."

"Ham again?!"

"I got sick once eating . . . but I think I'm pretty much over that now."

FAUX PAS AT WEDDINGS

"I hope this marriage lasts longer than his (her) last one."

"Thanks for giving the kids the nice silver tray. Unfortunately, they received three others just like it. Would you mind if they returned it?"

"His (her) ex was a lot better looking and had more money, too!"

"I wonder if she is . . . well you know. . . ."

FAUX PAS AT FUNERALS

"It's all for the best."

"She (he) couldn't have died at a worse (better) time."

"You'll get married (have another child, etc.), again."

"My husband's (wife's) illness was much worse."

"How much do you think the coffin cost?"

"I hope he left you a bundle."

"Funerals are such a waste of time and good flowers."

Speaking your mind at family gatherings may get a laugh, but if you're not careful, it might cause offense or even a family feud. These situations call for tact, listening and knowing when and what to say. By choosing the right words, communications with your relatives will be much smoother.

"Fate chooses your relations; you choose your friends."
—Jacques Delille, French poet, 1738–1813

Let's face it. Talking to the people you love is a real communication challenge. Your kids need reassurance, consistency and respect. Remember that they learn mostly by your examples—both good and bad. Listening to pushy parents and in-laws can decrease their desire to run your life. Aging parents want to maintain their independence but may need your help. Above all, remember good manners count, especially when talking to your relatives.

Now you have all the words, phrases, opening lines and examples you need to say the right thing in any situation. You will see that, with a little practice, you will be more confident and poised whenever and wherever you speak. Keep in mind that most people will respond positively to you if you are genuinely interested in what they say and respectful of their views. Finally, be yourself, show your sense of humor and remember these words of wisdom from Will Rogers: "Everything is funny, as long as it's happening to someone else."

INDEX

Page numbers in **bold** indicate boxed information.

Don Gabor helps companies who want people with effective communication skills and individuals who want to become better conversationalists. Don has written several books and audiotapes, including the best-seller, *How to Start a Conversation and Make Friends.* His customized programs show salespeople, executives, managers and staff how to improve their ability to communicate and achieve results.

For individuals who want personalized training, Don also offers one-on-one executive coaching for speeches, presentations and conversation skills. He has been presenting his programs to associations, businesses, colleges and corporations since 1980. Don was a spokesperson for Sprint and Frito-Lay.

Don is a member of the National Speakers Association and the American Society for Training and Development. He is a frequent media guest who *The New Yorker* called "a gifted conversationalist."

Please contact Don Gabor to receive a free conversation tip sheet and more information about his books, audiotapes, videos and workshops.

Telephone: 718-768-0824
Toll-free: 800-423-4203
Website: www.dongabor.com
E-mail: don@dongabor.com

Conversation Arts Media
P.O. Box 715
Brooklyn, NY 11215